STRATEGIES ⌐

A WEB 2.0
ENVIRONMENT

The true self is selfless.

Dharma Master Cheng Yen

STRATEGIES FOR BUILDING A WEB 2.0 LEARNING ENVIRONMENT

Chih-Hsiung Tu

LIBRARIES UNLIMITED

AN IMPRINT OF ABC-CLIO, LLC
Santa Barbara, California • Denver, Colorado • Oxford, England

Library of Congress Cataloging-in-Publication Data

Tu, Chih-Hsiung
Strategies for building a Web 2.0 learning environment / Chih-Hsiung Tu.
    pages cm.
  Includes bibliographical references and index.
    ISBN 978–1–59884–686–7 (pbk.) — ISBN 978–1–59884–687–4 (ebook) 1. Distance education—Computer-assisted instruction. 2. Internet in education. 3. Web 2.0—Study and teaching. 4. Inquiry-based learning. 5. Computer network resources. 6. Libraries and distance education. 7. Libraries and the Internet. I. Title.
LC5803.C65T8   2014
371.35′8—dc23   2013029815

ISBN: 978–1–59884–686–7
EISBN: 978–1–59884–687–4

18 17 16 15 14   1 2 3 4 5

This book is also available on the World Wide Web as an eBook.
Visit www.abc-clio.com for details.

Libraries Unlimited
An Imprint of ABC-CLIO, LLC

ABC-CLIO, LLC
130 Cremona Drive, P.O. Box 1911
Santa Barbara, California 93116-1911

This book is printed on acid-free paper ∞

Manufactured in the United States of America

To Gayle

CONTENTS

TU, CHIH-HSIUNG.

STRATEGIES FOR BUILDING A WEB 2.0 LEARNING
ENVIRONMENT.

Paper   169 P.

SANTA BARBARA: LIBRARIES UNLIMITED, 2014

AUTH: NORTHERN ARIZONA UNIV. GUIDEBOOK FOR
DISTANCE ED., CORPORATE TRAINERS, ETC.

LCCN 2013-29815

ISBN 1598846868   Library PO# AP-BOOKS

		List	50.00	USD
395 NATIONAL UNIVERSITY LIBRAR	Disc		.0%	
App. Date 1/15/14 SOE-EDU 8214-11	Net		50.00	USD

SUBJ: DISTANCE EDUCATION--COMPUTER-ASSISTED
INSTRUCTION.

CLASS LC5803   DEWEY# 371.358   LEVEL PROF

YBP Library Services

TU, CHIH-HSIUNG.

STRATEGIES FOR BUILDING A WEB 2.0 LEARNING
ENVIRONMENT.

Paper   169 P.

SANTA BARBARA: LIBRARIES UNLIMITED, 2014

AUTH: NORTHERN ARIZONA UNIV. GUIDEBOOK FOR
DISTANCE ED., CORPORATE TRAINERS, ETC.

LCCN 2013-29815

ISBN 1598846868   Library PO# AP-BOOKS

		List	50.00	USD
395 NATIONAL UNIVERSITY LIBRAR	Disc		.0%	
App. Date 1/15/14 SOE-EDU 8214-11	Net		50.00	USD

SUBJ: DISTANCE EDUCATION--COMPUTER-ASSISTED
INSTRUCTION.

CLASS LC5803   DEWEY# 371.358   LEVEL PROF

ILLUSTRATIONS

FIGURES

TABLES

PREFACE

I have been teaching online for more than 15 years. Six years ago, I was introduced to various Web 2.0 tools, such as blogs, wikis, social media, and so on. I saw the potential in implementing Web 2.0 tools to support on-line social interaction. Cautiously, I integrated an online discussion board into my online courses. Both my students and I had a positive experience, so I integrated additional tools into my existing learning management system (LMS). My students started asking, "Where is the content? The course instructions are all over the place. Do I need to learn so many tools? Why can't we just use BlackBoard?" Instead of complementing my teaching methods, the tools distracted and confused the students, who had a hard time utilizing them for coursework. I sat back and reflected on what I had done wrong. I asked myself, "Am I building a tower with duct tape?" I still thought it was valuable to integrate Web 2.0 to promote online social inter-action, so I consulted with my colleagues. They indicated that they had faced the same dilemmas and had decided that they should just integrate one or two tools. Some of them decided not to integrate the tools at all, since social media have such a negative reputation in some schools and school districts. Many teachers were afraid of being embarrassed because they lack knowl-edge in using social media. Frequently, the mass media report terrible results of younger people using social media. Therefore, the schools or school dis-tricts banned their use, because they believe that allowing access to social networks in school will expose students to potential risks, most notably cyberbullying (Blazer, 2012).

It seemed ironic that educators could foresee the potential of Web 2.0 tools yet avoid integrating them. I asked, "If it is not the tools, what went wrong?" If not the tools, it must be instructional paradigms and strategies.

I applied the wrong learning paradigm to require online learners to use certain tools. The key concept of Web 2.0 is "You," which means "learners" in the learning context. With so many Web 2.0 tools to choose from, and particularly since many are free, perhaps, I reasoned, we should allow learners to make their own selections of learning tools to achieve their learning goals, rather than have all use the same tools, such as LMS. By selecting relevant and effective tools, learners become engaged in creating their own personal learning environment to achieve their learning goals. This approach takes learning to a higher level of learner-centered learning. To online instructors, this is the most effective approach, and it involves more than the technology we have and their use (tools); it relates to how well we put things together (instructional strategies). In other words, educators today must look into effective, emerging "instructional strategies."

Web 2.0 tools have the potential to render the world flat; effective Web 2.0 instructional strategies can enable and catalyze this process. Educators do not play the role of sole content and knowledge authority anymore. In addition to listening to instructors and doing research, learners should be encouraged to create, to share, to manage, and to collaborate on their learning content with other learners.

I challenged myself to explore Web 2.0's network learning in comparing and contrasting online learning. I started working with my online master students in educational technology to co-design and co-teach an online course. As an instructor in this course, I laid out an outline for student groups to collaboratively develop open learning content. After the semester, students created a textbook for the course, and we used it for the upcoming semester. Since then, I have repeated the same instructional design for every semester. This course has resulted in more than 10 editions of the course textbook.

My students have reflected that the course instructional design and strategies were challenging, but they felt that their learning was more effective than through typical online instructions. They also indicated not only that they fulfilled their own learning goals in the course, but also that their learning was more meaningful. Additionally, they told me that their learning outcome became a useful contribution to the learning community. Their attitude was: we don't just take, we contribute as well. In fact, with the integration of open educational resources (OERs), many previous students returned to the class for online professional development training sessions, provided by the current students, for updates in the field.

I learned with my students. Gradually, I identified the concepts of personal learning environment (PLE) and open network learning environment (ONLE) that integrate network instructional strategies, such as participatory web, user-generated content (UGC), community-community interaction, aggregation, social content sharing, social tagging, mobile learning, social network and information visualization, and so on. Later these network instructional strategies were grounded as the open network linkage design model.

I was invited to deliver many keynote speeches on my open network learning integration. The audiences resonated their Web 2.0 integrations and practices with mine, and expressed that the concepts and the models of PLE and ONLE could be the solutions to using duct tape to build instructions Web 2.0 instruction. They suggested I write a book to support other educators interested in integrating Web 2.0 tools. Here it is!

Many concepts and designs and instructional strategies for PLE and ONLE originated from my online courses. My doctoral and master students worked collaboratively with me in the designs, integrations, practices, and research. I would like to express my appreciation to all my students.

PART I

BACKGROUND AND CONCEPTS

Part I includes two chapters, which discuss main concepts and constructs of PLE. This foundation allows readers to start building their understanding and knowledge in PLE and ONLE.

CHAPTER 1

Introduction

WEB 2.0 DISRUPTS LMS

Web 2.0 technologies have the potential to innovate current distance learning (Sharples, 2002). In fact, Weller (2007b), Mott and Wiley (2009), and Tu and Blocher (2010) have argued that Web 2.0 tools disrupt learning management systems (LMS) because LMS are *institutionally* controlled environments rather than teacher or learner constructed. LMS has been criticized for creating dependency rather than allowing autonomy for students (Powell, 2006) because it uses static resources and takes tasks out of context (Herrington et al., 2005), but, perhaps most importantly, it limits learners' focus on technology developments (Mott and Wiley, 2009). Web 2.0, on the other hand, offers students the ability to create and to personalize their own learning environments that are tailor-made to collaborate with others in a more open network environment.

Web 2.0 has become synonymous with a more interactive, user-generated, and collaborative Internet instrument (Alexander, 2006). Many argue that the new possibilities that these social networking tools present have resulted in a fundamental shift in the way students learn, consume, and produce new artifacts (Braun and Schmidt, 2000). Therefore, researchers value whether learners are given tools and opportunities to create personal learning environments to enhance their own learning (Tu, Blocher, and Roberts, 2008).

Web 2.0 learning technology offers more equity of participation and mutual negotiation than traditional learning methods and tools. Conole (2008) poses critical questions about the implementation of Web 2.0 tools into school curriculums: Will the changes in social practice we have seen generally through the adoption of Web 2.0 happen automatically, or is there something fundamentally different about education and learning? "Will simply letting 'Web 2.0' loose on education be enough to bring about such changes or is something more needed?" Current online learning technology, such as LMS, is essentially more individualistic and objective, while the philosophies inherent in Web 2.0 technology are more social and subjective. This book recommends and describes an open network linkage design model to assist educators and learners in constructing their personal learning environment (PLE) and open network learning environment (ONLE); and shows readers how to implement the necessary changes.

PARADIGM CHANGE

Moving from learning management system to personal learning environment and open network learning environment requires a fundamental shift in pedagogical paradigm and practice (van Harmelen, 2006a), from a culture of dependency and disempowerment of learners (Sclater, 2008) to promoting learners' autonomy (Powell, 2006); and from an institution-centered to a personalized social learning paradigm. Learning involves more than learning about content; it requires the learner to learn with content and to create and share effective learning environments. The innovative social learning paradigm is to create and share effective learning environments. The social learning paradigm engages learners in becoming competent global digital citizens in a "human network." It demands more than tool-based learning. Whiteman (2002) argued that effective learning reform happens when educators and instructors envision and organize themselves to support learning.

In this model, the instructor's responsibilities entail more than delivering content to learners, which decontextualizes learning; instead, the instructor needs to focus on the process of learning (Herrington, Reeves, and Oliver, 2005). In fact, content created by instructors or experts is often not appreciated by learners as context-rich content. Context-rich learning should be constructed, coconstructed, and shared by learners. The constructing and sharing process allows learners to self-organize learning resources, network with people, and connect through tools. Educators must gain an adequate understanding of the new social learning paradigm by not educating "knowledgeable" students but instead engaging them to become "knowledge-able" (Wesch, 2009) learners. To enable learners to construct and coconstruct learning, the learning environment should be open and allow social networking. That way, the learning constructed by learners is richer in context and more meaningful to the human network. The innovative social learning paradigm provides a greater opportunity for learning autonomy, diversity, openness, and connectedness (van Harmelen, 2006).

Creating a learning network to share also generates a sense of intimacy among the creator, the viewers, and the global community in the digital world (Campbell, n.d.). Learners do not just act as online learners; they also become "network" learners who are able to develop the agile minds of resourceful individuals (Clarke and Jennings, 2009), build interoperable learning infrastructure (Bush and Mott 2009), and master and manage the architecture for their learning environments.

ISSUES

An effective PLE and ONLE design model is greatly needed. The issues of integrating PLE and ONLE may originate in the inadequate perceptions of new paradigms and inappropriate integration. PLE and ONLE require conceptual model shifts in theory and practices. Norman (2008) described the dilemma educators and students face; PLE and ONLE require learners to build their own "centralized" learning environments in a "decentralized" distributed learning network. Without a strategic design for PLE and ONLE, network learning functions about as well as using duct tape to build a tower. What is needed is what Norman (2008) calls "eduglu," as a method for stitching different tools together.

The integration of ONLE requires more than just connecting technology. Fundamentally, it involves a paradigm shift. When educators integrate new and emerging ONLE to support teaching and learning, they too often apply old teaching paradigms to integrate and to design with ONLE. This results in applying gun barrel vision to view the world of new ideas. It is what Bush and Mott (2009) called "the tactical implementation of specific technologies which often simply automate the past" (p. 17). Multiple Web 2.0 tools frequently overwhelm learners and instructors; and their mechanical features diffuse and blur the importance of people, rather than technology and mechanics, as the center of a human network.

Ultimately, this approach results in negative teaching and learning experiences. Typically, learners and instructors access each Web 2.0 tool by visiting each tool website, because they perceive each tool as an individual entity and separate from other tools. When integrating any new tool in ONLE, learners and instructors see it as just another tool to use, another website to visit, and another account to log in to (Faculty Focus, 2009). Accessing all the required tools overwhelms learners and instructors; and, frequently, some tools are abandoned or forgotten. Indeed, the integration of multiple "Web 2.0 tools has created frustration among educators and students because they lack knowledge" (Tu et al., 2012, p. 13) needed to effectively operate the tools (Lee, Miller, and Newnham, 2008), because it is difficult to learn different tools (Weller, 2007a), because it is challenging to keep track of multiple authentications (Suess and Morooney, 2009), and because visiting multiple sites for different tools is tedious and time-consuming. "This phenomenon results from a lack of understanding of the social networking learning paradigm and inappropriate integration" (Tu et al., 2012, p. 13). ONLE's key features—and its advantage—lie in "internetworking and interlinking." This approach implies that the integrating of multiple tools requires linking and connecting resources, people, and tools rather than utilizing them separately.

WHY THIS BOOK?

The purpose of this book is to provide a comprehensive and effective guide for classroom teachers, at all levels, and trainers who are interested in integrating the concept of PLE and ONLE into their online instruction, or instruction that utilizes both face-to-face and online formats. Rather than dwelling on lofty theories, this book offers a design model, practical guidelines and examples that are based on current effective theories, well-grounded frameworks, and the extensive online teaching experiences of the author. The book is intended for use by practitioners in the field; however, researchers and others may find it useful as well, because the guidelines and activities discussed here have grown from many years of online teaching and are based on comprehensive research performed by the author.

This book is a good companion to *Twenty-One Designs to Build Online Collaborative Learning Community*, published by Libraries Unlimited in 2004 (www.abc-clio.com/product.aspx?isbn=9781591581550). While the 2004 book focuses on "online" instructional design and strategies, this book focuses on instructional designs and strategies to apply to "network learning technologies" to build advanced PLE and ONLE for all levels of educators.

Very few publications are available to provide educators, trainers, and instructional designers with the tools to develop effective PLE and ONLE. Those that are available deal primarily with programming and focus on technological information that is unnecessary and overwhelming to educators, trainers, and instructional designers. Additionally, there are no current publications targeted to educators that address the applications of social media in a learning environment.

For Educators

Traditional and online classroom teachers, corporate trainers, and instructional designers who are interested in integrating Web 2.0 tools completely or partially into their instruction will find this book useful. Any teacher who is interested in Web 2.0 instructions and integrations can apply the contents of this book immediately without the necessity of intensive reading, practical experience, or battling with technological terminologies. It can be used as a textbook for educators on subjects such as online instruction design, online learning design, distance education, and network learning environment.

For Professional References

The format of this book allows it to be used as a personal reference for classroom teachers, school administrators, online learning researchers, corporate trainers, corporate administrators, and those who are interested in the online learning environment.

For Researchers

Since the activities, guidelines, examples, and discussions are based on the current literature and research, researchers may find that this book provides a good case for the online collaborative learning community, PLE, and ONLE for future research and development.

WHAT WILL YOU LEARN FROM THIS BOOK?

Readers will learn the concepts of PLE and ONLE and the open network linkage design model. The design model covers and is divided into four dimensions (cognitive, social, network, and integration) and eight linkage designs (personal portal, RSS, third party, widget, social tagging, social network, mobile, and InfoViz).

The book is divided into six main parts:

- Part I Background and Designs
- Part II Social Dimension
- Part III Network Dimension
- Part IV Integration Dimension
- Part V Cognitive Dimension
- Part VI Comprehensive Integration

Part I includes two chapters that discuss the main concepts and constructs of PLE and ONLE. This foundation allows readers to start building their understanding and knowledge of PLE and ONLE. Part II guides network learners to project appropriate digital and social identities in the individual, social, and cultural environments. Part III provides open and network learning architectures structures to connect tools, humans, and environments. Part IV emphasizes social and collaborative community activities in ONLE instructional strategies. Part V emphasizes effective learning processes and development, placing the key instructions on creating, editing, sharing, and remixing learning content socially and collaboratively. Part VI presents a full-scale PLE and ONLE integration without using a learning management system and advances PLE and ONLE to another level of learning, global digital citizenship.

Chapter 2 provides the foundation of this book that lays the groundwork for the concepts of PLE and ONLE and suggests the open network linkage design model for building PLE and ONLE.

In chapter 3, readers learn how to present, manage, and organize digital social identities via online profiles. In face-to-face environments, most people are aware of the importance of presenting themselves. In online environments, due to the lack of immediate and real feedback channels from others, people lack knowledge in presenting their digital social identities. Inappropriate digital social identities can cause damage to personal public images and even raise concerns about safety and security.

In chapter 4, readers learn to integrate social networking design's friends, fans, followers, groups, and circles, community features to support community learning. Educators frequently overlook the value of social networking sites, such as Facebook and Twitter, to support learning because these sites are so often used for purely "social," "informal," or "casual" purposes, rather than as a learning tool. However, network learning group activities can easily be integrated to support a learning community in a smaller course community or on a larger scale, outside of schools.

Web 2.0 users are frequently overwhelmed by the large amount of online content. RSS and RSS readers are effective tools to assist users in managing and sharing their learning content. Chapter 5 covers the integration of RSS and RSS readers to manage, organize, and share "new" content in learning and classroom environments.

In chapter 6, readers explore the integration of "widgets" to enhance their learning communities. Most Web 2.0 tools have a widget feature to be displayed on other websites to make active connection. Strategically integrating widgets is critical to the success of network learning environments.

Through the integration of multiple Web 2.0 tools we commonly have multiple channels of resources to organize and manage. In chapter 7, readers learn to centralize scattered tools and functions into one tool, so all tools and sites synchronize via cloud computing technology.

Readers learn to integrate PLE tools to manage and monitor multiple Web 2.0 tools in chapter 8. When Web 2.0 tools are used to support teaching and learning, frequently multiple Web 2.0 tools are utilized, which requires the creation of multiple Web 2.0 accounts and multiple logins to these accounts. PLE tools can assist users in organizing and managing multiple Web 2.0 learning tools via gadgets.

In chapter 9, readers are shown how to integrate Web 2.0 tools into their mobile devices to achieve learning anywhere and at any time. Many Web 2.0 tools have "apps" for cell phones, such as Twitter viewing/posting, Delicious viewing/sharing, blog viewing/posting, and tweet to calendars, etc. With the integration of apps, learners and teachers are empowered to interact anywhere by phone.

Chapter 10 explores how to integrate flat-structured discussion boards to enhance students' critical thinking skills, such as the wiki discussion board, blog discussion board, and Twitter discussion board, etc. Traditionally, online discussion is conducted by threaded structure. Web 2.0's flat-structures can support higher critical-thinking skills and scaffold deeper learning.

In chapter 11, we focus on using social bookmarking tools to share distributed-learning resources. Effective social tagging to share distributed-learning resources with multiple communities is critical to educators and learners. Readers will learn to use tagging strategies to share with four different communities: community of interest, community of purpose, community of passion, and community of practice.

The web has gone beyond texts to support learning. In chapter 12, readers explore the application of information visualization to support teaching and learning instructions. Visual learning tools are new tools that provide different modes to support learning, such as using tag clouds to enhance and deepen understanding; using Wordle Arts to enhance and improve focus and meaningful writings; and using visual and spatial tools to present thinking and ideas.

Traditional online interaction occurs in text-based formats. In chapter 13, multimodality representation technology—such as VoiceThread, Vialogues, Twitter, and blogs—are explored as teaching and learning tools. Multimodality representation tools empower learners to select preferred modalities—media (such as text, audio, and/or visual) and tools (computer, telephone, and smartphone)—to present their thinking and ideas and to interact with other learners in different online activities (e.g., online discussion, storytelling, language learning, or drama learning activities).

ONLE integration can reach a large scale. In chapter 14, readers learn the comprehensive ONLE integrations by using multiple Web 2.0 tools to fully achieve online teaching and learning. Many educational institutions and schools lack the budget or manpower to integrate CMS (course management system) to fully support online learning. The chapter describes effective multiple Web 2.0 tools that can deliver network learning content and engage network learners and teachers in active and interactive learning.

The last chapter, chapter 15, summarizes what has been covered in previous chapters and discusses potential issues that can arise, such as mental model shifts, support, safety and security, whether teachers and learners are ready for new paradigms, requiring a longer process, and requiring intensive facilitation. Additionally, global digital citizenship is discussed in terms of transforming from online learners to network learners and finally global digital citizens.

Portions of chapters 2 and 10 were previously published by Chih-Hsiung Tu, Laura Sujo-Montes, Cherng-Jyh Yen, Junn-Yih Chan, and Michael Blocher in *TechTrends* for chapter 2; and by Chih-Hsiung Tu, Michael

Blocher, and Lawrence Gallagher in *Journal of Educational Technology Development and Exchange,* for chapter 10.

HOW TO USE THIS BOOK

Each chapter is explained from three-dimensional connections (tools, resources, and people), as well as covering design concepts and guidelines, design activities, linkage designs, relevant tools, practical network instructional examples illustrated by the case studies, and collaborative-shared social bookmark resources with social tagging scheme. The purpose of these practices is for you to build effective PLE and ONLE that afford online learners opportunities to create, manage, organize, aggregate, and share their own PLEs within human networks through this design model.

Each of the design concepts and guidelines is presented from four vantage points: how to select, how to organize, how to share/collaborate, and how to link. When integrating each linkage design or strategy, readers are encouraged to contemplate how this linkage and strategy may apply to these four activities. "To select," consider how to select relevant tools to deliver the linkage and strategy; "to organize," plan how to organize the linkage and strategy to achieve learning and teaching needs and goals; "to share/collaborate," think about how to engage learners in sharing and collaborating with learning resources, tools, and human networks; and "to link," ponder how to link multiple tools together to strengthen PLE and ONLE.

Design activities are included to help readers learn what types of learning activities can be integrated to support each linkage design and strategy. Effective design activities are listed in the last part of each chapter. Readers are urged to follow the design concept and guidelines to create their own creative learning activities and share their design activities with other readers by tagging to share the resources.

Each linkage design strategy is not meant to be a stand-alone enabler. It is recommended that you always consider linking one linkage to other linkage designs. The open network linkage design model is not single-dimensional; rather it is a multidimensional road guide to help you design PLE and ONLE. It is important for you to challenge yourself with how you can link from one linkage to other ones.

In each chapter, one or more case studies are presented to help you comprehend how and what specific linkage design can be integrated into instructional activities. These suggested case studies can be adopted by following the instructions completely or partially.

All the tools, resources, content, or literature mentioned in each chapter are tagged with specific tags as social bookmarks on Delicious.com; therefore, you do not need to reresearch or retype the URL. Additionally, it is

Table 1.1 Social Tagging for Each Book Chapter

Chapter	Name	Tags
	Whole Book	SONLE (Strategies for Open Network Learning Environments)
1	Introduction	SONLE
2	Concepts of PLE and ONLE	SONLE, ONLE, PLE
3	Devise Digital Identity	SONLE, DI
4	Learn to Be a Butterfly on Social Networks	SONLE, SNL
5	Accrue RSS Linkage	SONLE, RSS
6	Believe in the Wonder of Widgets	SONLE, Widget
7	Discover the Hidden Power of Third-Party Linkage	SONLE, 3rdParty
8	Construct Your PLE	SONLE, PLE
9	Mobilize Your Learning	SONLE, ML
10	Make Your World Flat	SONLE, FD
11	Tag to Touch Your Community	SONLE, Social, Tagging
12	Erase the Invisibility	SONLE, InfoViz
13	Go beyond Texts	SONLE, MMR
14	Innovate to Create	SONLE, ONLE, PLE
15	Finis	SONLE, ONLE, PLE

recommended that you share your relevant online resources with other readers by bookmaking them on Delicious with the designed social tags; in this way, the chapter resources become a living and organic environment while you and other readers add additional resources to each chapter.

Table 1.1 is the overview of design tags for the book and each chapter, which offer you another way to look at and access the content.

To achieve the deepest understanding, it is recommended that you first read from the beginning to the end to obtain an overview of this book. You can then select a chapter of interest to plan and design your own PLE and ONLE instructions and activities. If you cannot read the entire book, first read chapter 2 to obtain a good understanding of PLE and ONLE framework and models; then read the chapters that address the topics of greatest interest to you.

BACKGROUND

The framework, concepts, model, guidelines, instructions, and strategies recommended in this book are based on current theoretical frameworks and constructs in open network learning, recent studies, recent publications, and the practices that have been successful in the online classes this author designs and teaches. The content presented is derived from lessons learned from teaching online courses and experiences gleaned in online classrooms. The author's professional career has developed through technology and the use of an online learning environment. This book is based on the belief that sharing our experiences in online instructional design and online teaching provides excellent resources to those who are interested in personal learning environments and open network learning environments.

CHAPTER 2

Concepts of PLE and ONLE

EMERGING LEARNING CONCEPT

Network learning technologies, such as social media and Web 2.0, have emerged as new learning tools for creative, interactive, and collaborative learning. Researchers observe two new critical learning movements to advance learning to a more innovative point: learners should be granted freedom to access, create, and recreate their learning content, and prospects to go beyond a formal learning system to connect and to interact with global digital communities (Siemens and Matheos, 2010). Dede (2008) has argued that the most effective strategy for learning is to integrate multiple technologies and learning tools instantaneously rather than a single learning system, such as educational institutions' formal learning management system (LMS). Therefore, educators should integrate open educational resources (OER) in social and networked learning environments via various Web 2.0 technologies. In other words, social, open, and network are the key aspects. Tu et al. (2012) claimed effective integration with open, social networking tools would instigate an ultimate shift from the way students consume content to students create, recreate, and remix learning content into new content.

Ultimate learning goals for Web 2.0 technology integration require learners with strong learner-centered knowledge and the ability to construct their own PLE in an effective ONLE. Learners, educators, and administrators face a new

Portions of this chapter were previously published by Chih-Hsiung Tu, Laura Sujo-Montes, Cherng-Jyh Yen, Junn-Yih Chan, and Michael Blocher, "The Integration of Personal Learning Environments and Open Network Learning Environments," *TechTrends*, 56(3) 2012. Used with kind permission from Springer Science+Business Media.

dilemma with Web 2.0 integration because new network learning disrupts a traditional paradigm, taking them from more teacher- and institution-centered teaching and learning to a more personalized, open, social system, based on network applications and collaboration. It is inevitable that educators can build sound instructional ONLE to facilitate and to engage learners in creating their PLEs. Therefore, the new learning paradigm is personalized and individualized yet also communicative, interactive, and collaborative.

PERSONAL LEARNING ENVIRONMENT

Network learners, empowered by open, social, and network technologies, personalize their digital learning environments by connecting, organizing, and managing their three learning networks—content, people, and technology—resulting in PLEs. Tu et al. (2012, p.14) concluded that "by appropriating a range of tools, and by connecting people, resources, and tools," they are able to meet their learning interests and needs.

PLE involves three strategic notions (van Harmelen, 2006b): that learners are able to construct personal learning objectives and goals; that they are able to manage learning content, tools, and processes; and that they can communicate effectively with others to achieve learning goals. With the freedom and flexibility of building personalized learning, a PLE frequently builds on multiple learning networks, learning systems, tools, or technologies. Siemens (2007, para. 2) described PLE as "a collection of tools, brought together under the conceptual notion of openness, interoperability, and learner control." This can be achieved by applying a personalized portal (e.g., with Symbaloo, iGoogle, Google Reader) to collect and organize different Web 2.0 tools and technologies into a central site; this allows learners to access their learning content, tools, and people networks without visiting each individual site.

A successful PLE is created through accessing technologies, or tools. Personalizing, appropriating, and managing learning goals, learning values, and learning technologies are the keys to effective PLEs. Conole (2008) contended students would often avoid the learning tools provided by their educational institutions if they didn't find them useful or relevant to their digital learning. Instead, students seek their preferred learning tools, particularly those that allow them to personalize the tools. Additionally, effective PLEs require students to understand their learning needs, objectives, and, goals; and to appropriate relevant learning content, tools, and people networks. In other words, the PLE principles are grounded in connecting people networks, tool networks, and recourse networks to construct an "environment."

OPEN NETWORK LEARNING ENVIRONMENT

Open network learning environments built and facilitated by instructors and educators are essential to enable network learners to construct their

PLEs. Tu et al. (2012, p. 14) stated, "ONLE is a digital environment that empowers learners to participate in creative endeavors, conduct social networking, organize and reorganize social contents, and manage social acts by connecting people, resources, and tools by integrating Web 2.0 tools to design environments that are totally transparent, or open to public view." This open, transparent, socially networked architecture is the critical blueprint to educators to promote PLEs within ONLEs.

ONLE, as an organic entity, is entwined around a "human network" that also contains content and tools. PLE and ONLE engage network learners to transform information consumers to learning content contributors and creators; to expand from individuals to more specific sociocultural interaction; and to extend from individual creations to more cooperative and collective co-constructions. Social constructivism accentuates a wider range of community knowledge co-constructions to support the value of each individual's uniqueness. In ONLE, all individuals are considered experts in some sense, and all community members and their contributions are part of the social network and environments. Therefore, effective ONLE should be capable of encompassing a complicated and constant influx of knowledge contributed by a multitude of individual members. In other words, effective ONLE architectures and designs enable members to build their own PLE, and to grow as a community through the organic designs of open, social, and network scaffolds.

What immediately becomes apparent about Web 2.0 tools in ONLE is that many are multifaceted. Their use in combination leads to a new simplicity in the system; learning resources can be transmitted seamlessly between systems, and functionality created in one tool can be embedded or be made available in another (Conole, 2008). A multifaceted learning environment is a network instruction that focuses on learning content in addition to a learning tool network and a human network. Therefore, a learning network allows network learners to build their resources and human networks through their learning tool network, such as using Twitter to weave together human and resource networks, or using mobile devices to organize learning apps. Twitter allows one to follow individuals who possess important resources that can be accessed on any mobile device. It is common for educators to integrate multiple Web 2.0 tools to support learning, such as wiki, blog, Facebook, and Twitter. Dede (2008) argued that the most effective instructional approach allows learners to analyze the nature of their own learning and to integrate multiple tools simultaneously to support their PLE.

The new learning should move away from a centralized learning system to a more distributed personal learning environment that allows these separate tools to be easily aggregated in one place. PLE is more self-directed and collaboration-oriented learning where individual learners construct their own learning agendas and roadmap to fulfill their own learning goals. These engagements support interactive learning activity, learning ownership, and responsibility.

It is evident now that ONLE enables individuals to personalize the environment in which they learn, appropriating a range of tools to meet their interests and needs. In ONLE, learners are empowered with personal portals, such as iGoogle and mobile apps, to organize and manage their preferred learning tools, such as cloud e-mails and Google Docs rather than MS Word, to meet their needs. Research examining how students are appropriating technologies describes similar changes in practice: students are mixing and matching different tools to meet their personal needs and preferences. Learners should not be seen as tool operators (Weller, 2010); they should be engaged in building positive social and digital identities to enrich network connections and learning networks. Network tools are able to capture and record connections and interactions as digital cognition prints that contribute additional value to other network learners. The learning concepts of PLE and ONLE are based on a decentralized model that emphasizes what Weller (2010) argued: quality, flexibility, pedagogical suitability, relevance, educator control, and personalization. In other words, PLE and ONLE are open to interested parties in principle, but may reasonably be secured to collaborators in practice.

Framework and Constructs

Siemens's "Connectivism" (2005) and Tu, Blocher, and Roberts's (2008) "Constructs for Web 2.0 Learning Environments" set forth two main theoretical concepts for integrating PLE and ONLE. Siemens (2005, para. 19) articulates learning as "a process that occurs within nebulous environments of shifting core elements." More specifically, he argued that learning should be based on "rapidly altering foundations ... [C]urrency (accurate, up-to-date knowledge) is the intent of all connectivist learning activities" (Siemens, 2005, para. 19). Obtaining the skills and knowledge in learning content and acquiring the skills and knowledge in connecting and linking to learning content are of equal importance. Siemens (2005) asserts the conduit or pipe is far more critical than the content.

Tu, Blocher, and Roberts (2008, p. 257) described constructs for Web 2.0 learning environments as substantiated in "socio-cultural learning, which is in a constant flux of cognitive development with the force of dynamic social interaction." Four dimensions constitute this construct: cognitive, social, networking, and integration. The cognitive dimension emphasizes effective learning process and development, placing the key instructions on creating, editing, sharing, and remixing learning content socially and collaboratively. Social learning provides a community playground to engage network learners to assume appropriate digital identities in individual, social, and cultural environments. Networking mechanisms scaffold open and network learning architectures to connect and link tools, people, and environments. Integration procedures escalate each individual member's social and collaborative community constructions and activities.

OPEN NETWORK LINKAGE DESIGN MODEL

An open network linkage design model for PLE and ONLE supports effective ONLE and PLE integration, and is therefore recommended. This model refers to a "linkage architecture" that "links and connects" multiple network resources, network learners, and Web 2.0 tools in ONLE to allow learners, instructors, and other ONLE stakeholders to construct and share their PLEs within a human network. This model's linkage architecture can resolve the issues of learning different tools, multiple authentications, visiting multiple sites, and tools to improve the effectiveness of PLE and ONLE.

The open network linkage design model for PLE and ONLE constitutes eight network linkages:

- Personal portal linkage
- Widget linkage
- RSS linkage
- Third-party linkage
- Social tagging linkage
- Social network linkage
- Mobile linkage
- InfoViz linkage (see Figure 2.1)

This linkage design model focuses on soft architecture design in terms of how to interlink multiple resources, people, and tools effectively to enhance PLE and ONLE, in addition to hard architecture, that is, the technologies' mechanical features.

Using this type of design model guides learners and instructors to obtain linkage skills and knowledge to design and develop their PLE and ONLE. By combining this design model with competent linkage skills and knowledge, learners and instructors can evaluate any Web 2.0 tools, select appropriate tools for their learning and teaching, design and develop their PLE and ONLE, and assess their existing PLE and ONLE in order to improve them, and so on.

Personal Portal Linkage

Personal portal linkage is a customized portal technology that links multiple web 2.0 tools in one location and allows learners and instructors to manage their learning content, information, and communications. Learners can create a personal portal account with sites such as iGoogle and add any other learning tools or other related gadgets, such as Twitter, Google

Figure 2.1   Open Network Linkage Design Model

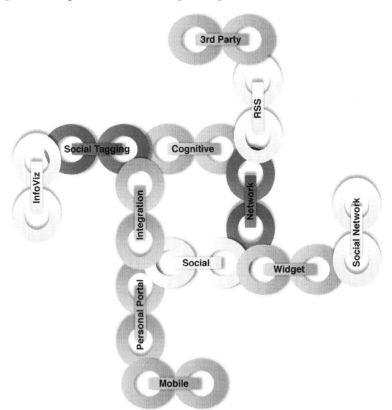

Calendar, Gmail, Google Docs, and others to the portal (see Figure 2.2). This technology is not limited to iGoogle. Learners can select different portal technologies, such as Google Reader, mobile devices, and Netvibes, to achieve the same functions. Additionally, learners should be encouraged to constantly monitor, evaluate, add or delete, edit, and manage their personal portal so that it reflects and speaks to their learning needs and learning goals.

Widget Linkage

Widget linkage refers to a stand-alone that can be embedded into another tool by learners or instructors on a webpage where they have rights of authorship (e.g., a webpage, blog, or profile on a social media site). This linkage empowers learners and instructors to access network resources based on their preferences rather than to navigate away from their portal sites to visit each

Figure 2.2   Personal Portal Linkage on iGoogle

tool site. Most Web 2.0 tools have features that allow users to obtain widget or embedded scripts and embed them into other webpages without requiring special technical skills. Frequently, all users need to do is to copy and paste the codes or scripts. By enabling this linkage, learners and instructors can connect people, resources, and tools to online instruction. Learners can obtain access to different information by selecting and embedding different widgets into their preferred webpages. For example, they can get video, other web pages, RSS feeds, survey, voting, clock, calendar, weather, calculator, news, and more by simply installing widgets. In other words, webpages can be transformed into mash-ups, and aggregate learning content and resources. Learners can access their chosen resources more easily and quickly in these personalized formats.

RSS Linkage

RSS linkage refers to the application of an RSS feed from one tool to others so learners can monitor or track a single place to get updates through live feeds. RSS (RDF site summary, rich site summary, or really simple syndication) is simple XML syntax for portraying recent additions of content to a website. It allows online learners to independently subscribe to their choice of content and sources across the web, thereby reducing the need for users to visit many individual websites.

For the retrieval of RSS feeds, users depend on RSS aggregators. There are a number of these available online as well as downloadable client-based and browser-based applications, such as Google Reader, Internet browsers, and MS Outlook. RSS feed is a format for delivering regularly changing web content. Many websites, such as blogs and news-related sites, are embedded with an RSS feed feature that allows readers to "subscribe." Users receive the updated feed content by visiting the RSS feed aggregator, such as Outlook E-mail, Internet browsers (Firefox, Internet Explorer, Chrome, Safari), Google Reader, and FeedReader. Users easily stay informed by retrieving the latest content from the multiple sites. It is more efficient to access content by accessing one location rather than visiting each site individually. Feed can be related to website content updates, blog updates, newspaper and journal articles, announcements, news, and database updates. RSS linkage provides many advantages to learners and instructors.

RSS linkages allow learners to track and organize the information and instructions they receive by category. Learners make an active decision to access information and instructions rather than having it presented directly to them. They have a chance to select, organize, and manage preferred RSS feeds to create their PLE. For example, learners can subscribe to Twitter, Delicious or Diigo (social bookmarking tools), newspaper, or magazine websites to their PLE; therefore, learners only need to access their PLE to receive any updated network learning content and resources, without visiting each individual RSS site. In this sense, RSS linkage design is related to constructivism. It is because of this relationship that Siemens (2007) states that learning is a network forming and connecting process with critical decision-making involved.

Third-Party Linkage

Third-party linkage refers to the application of third-party tools (such as Google Sync, Google Cloud Connect for Microsoft Office, Twitterfeed, TwitterDeck, Permalink, Google +, Patchlife, Posterous) to link multiple Web 2.0 tools, so content or resources can be streamed from one tool to others. Generally, a third-party linkage tool works behind the scenes; therefore, it is not apparent to users.

With Twitterfeed, learners and instructors can e-mail their message postings to the course blog without visiting the course blog; and these course blog postings are fed to the course Facebook page and course Twitter account while tweets are fed to the course schedule (Dipity). The same messages can be e-mailed for posting to multiple instructional networks. The initial process involves a simple e-mail, so learners and instructors can perform and access this linkage from their smartphones. Additionally, Posterous, a blog tool, can be considered a third-party linkage because it integrates an automatic posting to other social media tools such as Flickr, Twitter, and

Facebook. Third-party linkage can support learners and instructors in better social network content management and organization. It eliminates duplicated postings and tedious multiple tool usages.

Social Tagging Linkage

Social tagging linkage refers to social tags that link relevant content, networked friends/fans, and community. Many tools have social tagging features, such as Delicious, Flickr, Diigo, blog postings, and wiki discussion postings. Effective social tagging can increase learner-content, as well as learner-leaner, learner-instructor, and community-community interactions. Students can use tagging schemes to tag and share their online learning resources with other learners. These tags can be related to course number, instructional units, learning content, assignments, group units, and so on. Some examples of tags are EDU647, Lesson1, Module1, Assignment3, Team1, and Final Project. For example, if a student wants to tag the final project resource to share with his/her group 2 in the course ENG100, the resources can be tagged as ENG100, Group2, Final Project. With these tags, others can access the shared resource precisely.

With the effective tagging linkage, students have access to current and previous students' online learning resources. Social tagging linkage can achieve community-community interaction and community learning (community that learns) via effective social tagging architectures, because current students can access the tagged resources shared by previous students, while upcoming students can access the current class's tagged resources.

Hashtag is another method of social tagging. Hashtag refers to a word or phrases prefixed with the symbol "#" (i.e., hashtag). A hashtag has the function of creating groupings on Twitter. This enables tweets to be categorized based on a particular topic. In the case of online classes, students can tweet the course by the course number or other unique tags (e.g., #EDU777, #AECT, #ICEM) so that they do not have to follow each other for communication on Twitter. They can also easily follow the instructional activities via hashtags. Hashtags provide useful contexts and cues to support the learning community when they are integrated strategically and effectively. Learners and instructors can apply course hashtags to tweet course-related communication, such as soliciting support from the course community in real time rather than e-mailing. Learners and instructors can access updated Twitter feeds of the hashtag on mobile devices to achieve better mobile learning and ubiquitous learning.

Social Network Linkage

Social network linkage refers to learners connecting to online social networks by becoming friends or fans of others, or following others via Web

2.0 tools to build social relationships and to get updated on friends' learning resources and so forth. By becoming members of social networks, users are granted privileges to view more of their friends' resources and their social networks. By viewing the networks of their friends, users can identify more people who have the same or similar interests and expand their learning network. Instructors can also proactively engage learners and community members to network with others. Group and community members should become friends, fans, and followers to strengthen their social networking linkage power. Social network linkage generally is available on social network sites, such as Facebook, Twitter, LinkedIn, and MySpace; however, this linkage is not limited to social network sites. Many other Web 2.0 tools—such as Ning, wikis, and blogs—have social network linkage features as well, since Web 2.0 tools generally require users to have accounts. This allows users to build their profile and social network with other users within the same Web 2.0 tools.

Social network sites are not inherently social until social network linkage is established. Social network sites can be vital in providing channels for informal and unstructured learning (Selwyn, 2009). They can also help learners feel socially connected, which is a key factor to online course success and enables the development of group social structure and continued social interactions among individuals in an educational environment (Slagter van Tyron, and Bishop, 2009). Social network linkage encourages users "to establish and maintain relationships, to collaborate, to share thoughts and ideas, and in doing so create a 'socially connected' Web, where anyone can contribute and share knowledge freely" (Charlton, Devlin, and Drummond, 2009, p. 277). In other words, Social network linkage connects learners, supports different communities of practices (Conole and Culver, 2010), and creates a community of inquiry that motivates learning experiences and independent learning experiences for better employability (Jones, Blackey, Fitzgibbon and Chew, 2010).

Mobile Linkage

Mobile linkage refers to using mobile apps to link to Web 2.0 tools on mobile devices. Mobile linkage involves more than using an Internet browser to access online information. Specifically, by employing mobile apps, it focuses on controlling social context awareness, managing location-based communication, personalized multilayered interactivity, and optimized digital and social identities.

Mobile information and communication technologies are important enablers of the new social structure. The instructions built within Web 2.0 tools, such as iTunes U, Twitter, Delicious, Facebook, RSS, blogs, Google Apps, and so on can be accessed via mobile apps on mobile devices. Mobile learning is able to achieve something that traditional desktop or laptop computers cannot. Mobile linkage becomes more powerful when mobile devices are equipped with recording, camera, and Global Positioning System (GPS) technologies.

InfoViz Linkage

Information visualization (InfoViz) or InfoGraphic refers to information design that "uses pictures, symbols, colors, and words to communicate ideas, illustrate information, or express relationships visually" (Emerson, 2008, p. 4). Research has concluded that InfoViz supports learning in problem solving (Ware, 2004); knowledge acquisition (Keller et al., 2005); decision making (Chi, 2002; Spencer, 2007); understanding inaccessibly large amounts of data (Ware, 2004); recognizing unanticipated associations among data (Ware, 2004); discovering new explanations (Tufte, 1997); forming hypothesis about observed relationships (Ware, 2004); reducing cognitive load (Perkins, 1993); sense making (Chi, 2002); and allowing technology to support knowledge co-construction (Perkins, 1993).

Effective InfoViz linkage design should include six aspects (Card, Mackinlay, and Shneiderman, 1999):

- Memory and processing capabilities
- Information search paths
- Pattern detection
- Critical information
- Inferences
- Data manipulations

The available tools include Wordle, tag clouds, word clouds, Easel.ly, Dipity, and Memolane, as well as others.

PART II

SOCIAL DIMENSION

Part II guides network learners to project appropriate digital and social identities in individual, social, and cultural environments.

CHAPTER 3

Devise Digital Identity

Have you ever:

- Heard others were hurt on social network sites, such as Facebook?
- Thought about what your digital identity and digital social identity are?
- Considered whether your digital social identity depicts your ideal identity?

DIGITAL IDENTITY DESIGN CONCEPTS

Social network sites (SNSs) connect people and support different communities of practice (Conole and Culver, 2010). "The openness and malleability of use of these tools empowers users to express themselves to others, and to take part in shared activities, in a variety of contexts" (Hall, 2009, p. 30). "The orientation of SNSs towards self-presentation, the viewing of others' personal information, and multiple means of communication and exchange [have] certainly proved attractive to students" in educational settings (Selwyn, 2009, p. 158).

According to Jones, Blackey, Fitzgibbon, and Chew (2010), students also prefer to use educational technology for learning because they enjoy the use of technologies and online activities, they need more communications platform with peers, and they need peer sharing and encouragement. Social media provide "both educators and students with further connection and communication with each other or with people outside the classroom; and it provides a flexible environment for learner participation" (Jones, Blackey, Fitzgibbon, and Chew, 2010, p. 776). In fact, Ellison, Steinfield, and Lampe

(2007) found that intense users of SNS correlated with a sense of increased social belonging to college students. Zhao and Kuh (2004) verified that students who use SNS perceived that they were socially connected to their communities and performed better academically.

Social network sites are web-based services—such as Facebook, Twitter, LinkedIn, and blogs—that "allow individuals to construct a public or semi-public profile within a bounded system, communicate with a list of other users with whom they share a connection, and view and traverse their list of connections and those made by others within the system" (Boyd and Ellison, 2007, para. 5). Selwyn (2009) indicated that "SNSs are personal and personalizable spaces for online conversations and sharing of content based typically on the maintenance and sharing of 'profiles' where individual users can represent themselves to other users through the display of personal information, interests, photographs, social networks and so on" (p. 157). This social content sharing and interaction constitute a unique digital social identity for each participant and enables them to articulate and make their digital social identity visible to others in their social network (Boyd and Ellison, 2007).

Digital identities are the fundamental elements for social learning in social networking environments. Development of a digital identity and digital social identity are considered an opportunity to make learning more personally meaningful, collaborative, socially relevant, and contextually richer. Educators often view digital identity as an "optional" identity that represents their social and professional images, and that is not for teaching and learning. Educators have been unclear how digital identities may support their classroom teaching (Greenhow, Robelia, and Hughes, 2009) and typically overlook or ignore the uses of SNSs or social media. When it comes to their own digital social identities, educators generally create and share fairly simple and basic digital contents, often without knowing it. These misconceptions generally come from lacking or confusing the knowledge and skills of digital social identity, SNSs, and social media's technical notions.

If educators do not have an accurate understanding of digital identity and competent digital literacy, how can they provide, model, and scaffold classroom teachers with the correct understanding of digital identity or gain digital literacy? Without competent digital literacy to build appropriate digital identities, teachers will be unable to assist learners, particularly young learners, to justify and manage the needs for "risk-taking, role-playing, and creativity with the need for integrity and authenticity in their network learning experiences" (Greenhow, Robelia, and Hughes, 2009, p. 252).

Digital presentations and informal learning activities are familiar to young learners who have been writing about and sharing their feelings online, and these young learners are generally adept at digital presentations. Stern (2007) argued that youth "seek out the cathartic benefits of digital expression through art, music, or photography" (p. 96). These digital behaviors are generally seen by schools, teachers, and parents as a distraction to learning and risky or unsafe. Classroom teachers often even feel frightened of and do not know how to contend with SNS. Many schools and districts simply ban access to social network technologies on campus (Blazer, 2012). Teachers are in the front line of those who educate young learners; and they need to know how to guide students to enact their digital citizenship appropriately, how to "negotiate different online spaces and how to ascertain what information" (Greenhow, Robelia, and Hughes, 2009, p. 252) should be kept private. These teachers must learn about the development and management of digital identities on SNS, to adequately instruct and guide students. There are two types of online identities: digital identity and digital social identity. Digital identities are created voluntarily and involuntarily, since many actions and activities are recorded in digital forms and can be retrieved online without one actually being created. Our physical footprints—not just digital footprints—are imprinted on the digital world. The records of property ownership, telephone numbers, meeting participation, memberships, and social activities are stored indefinitely and can be retrieved online as an individual's digital identity. Others can easily view these digital records and footprints without the owner's awareness. What is the identity you wish to have in the digital world?

In this chapter, we discuss how to create and to manage digital identities via online profiles and digital social identities via social content sharing and social conversations on social networking sites.

DIGITAL IDENTITY DEVELOPMENT GUIDELINES

To Select Digital Identities

With the features of temporal and other special differences, online users can own multiple digital identities and digital social identities simultaneously. These are different from identities in the physical world. A digital identity may or may not represent one's real identity in the physical world. Educators and students should identify and select their ideal digital identities for their digital world.

There are three main types of digital identities, professional, social, and personal. For educators and students, a professional identity is related to their respective teaching and learning professions—for example, teacher, students, colleagues, associates, administrators. Your social identity represents your social life, such as the relationship you have with a wide circle of friends. Personal identity refers to the role you have with family and close friends. These different identities may or may not overlap in your real life. It depends on your own preferences, perceptions, and contexts. Some feel teacher-student relationships should be professional and should never be social or personal at all; while some perceive the issue differently. It is critical for you to determine what identity or identities you prefer to clearly represent yourself in the digital world.

To Organize Digital Identity

Manage your digital identity strategically and regularly, regardless of whether it represents your real identity or how you manage your real identity in the physical world. To a certain degree, people do have preferences on what identity they like to assume in their life. Digital identity management is also called "self-presentation." This becomes particularly critical when you choose to have more than one digital identity. Many unpleasant and destructive incidents have been experienced by educators on SNSs because inappropriate digital identities were presented to the wrong groups of social networks. For example, presenting personal identity to professional networks can be problematic. If one prefers to project a professional digital identity, sharing too many personal pictures or comments, such as pictures of drinking at a beach party, may not meet the original intention because it is perceived as sharing information that is too personal and does not align with a professional identity.

To Share and Collaborate on Digital Identity

Effective digital identities require more thought than just creating and developing; you must consider how and with whom you share them in different social networks as digital social identities. Clearly your professional identity is shared in your professional network, while your social identity should be presented to your social networks. Be sure to scrutinize your SNSs' profiles and your shared social content and communications to ensure that your preferred identity is presented to the intended networks. It is vital to update digital profiles regularly. When you have new or recent professional pictures, achievements, participations, recognitions, or new professional networks, it is necessary to update your profiles to reflect your current professional status and engagement. For professional social identities, you can post and share your professional reading resources, reflections, and comments to show you are actively engaged in the field.

To Link Tools to Digital Identity

Linking your preferred profiles and shared content to the correct SNSs is critical. Although SNSs are created for social networking in general, some sites cater to specific social networks. Generally speaking, Facebook, Twitter, and Google Circles are used as personal social networks, while LinkedIn is considered a professional network. Therefore, develop a professional identity for LinkedIn. For social networks that can be used as either professional or personal networks, like Facebook, Twitter, and Google Circles, clearly identify which social networks you intend to network with and develop relevant identities for them accordingly.

DIGITAL IDENTITY DESIGNS

To Create Digital Identity Activities

If you are an instructor, create and develop your SNS's profiles before you integrate any SNS into your instruction and encourage your students to use it. Instructors should also:

- Assist students in creating and managing their SNS profiles.
- Help students to social network with their classmates or others for learning purposes.
- Initiate posts and share social content on social media.
- Encourage students to post and share social content on social media.

LINKAGE DESIGNS FOR DIGITAL IDENTITY

Below are a few suggestions regarding the application of each linkage to enhance your digital identity instructions.

- *Personal portal linkage*: Add social network sites to your personal portal so you can participate in, monitor, edit, and update your status and profiles without visiting the social network sites.
- *RSS linkage*: Many social network sites have RSS feed features. You can subscribe to their RSS feeds, such as Twitter and LinkedIn.
- *Widget linkage*: Most social network sites have a widget feature that you can embed to any webpage.
- *Social tagging linkage*: Most social network sites have social tagging features, which allow you to organize and collaborate with others. See the chapter resources for the social tagging instructions for Facebook, Twitter (hashtag), and LinkedIn.
- *Mobile linkage*: Almost all social network sites have mobile apps for mobile devices on different platforms, Android, Blackberry, iOS, and so on. With mobile apps, you can access social network sites anywhere and anytime to manage your digital and social identities.
- *InfoViz linkage*: Many special applications allow users to create InfoViz based on their social network sites' activities, feeds, or social relationships. By analyzing these InfoViz, you can view the patterns and relations that you may not see in a normal format. See the

chapter resources for the InfoViz instructions for Facebook, Twitter (hashtag), and LinkedIn.

**LEARNING ACTIVITY:
PRESENTING APPROPRIATE AND
PROFESSIONAL DIGITAL IDENTITIES**

Purpose: To create ideal digital identity by crafting social networking profiles and sharing relevant network content.

Instructions: In this learning activity, you will create and manage appropriate and professional digital identities and digital social identities for social networking sites, social media, and Web 2.0 tools by creating and managing digital personal profiles and sharing appropriate social contents.

**Case I:
Crafting Digital Personal Profiles Like Celebrities**

On SNSs, every user is like a celebrity because all digital activities are recorded and can be made public. The activity here is called "who is who" and will engage students in crafting their digital profiles and ask them to guess which profile belongs to which classmate.

- The instructor should create his or her digital profile before the students do theirs.
- Define your digital identity: professional, personal, or social. For teaching and learning purposes, a professional digital profile is more appropriate for a teacher-student social network.
- Craft the profile: A typical profile includes different sections: Basic information, profile picture, photo albums, hobby/interests, and so on.
  - Basic information (name, gender, and date of birth): As a teacher, you may want to consider disclosing only basic personal information, such as your real name, education, and professional contact information. Regarding gender and date of birth, many SNSs allow you to make that information public or private. If you have younger students, consider using pseudonyms and make all basic personal information private, or avoid disclosing it at all for privacy and safety concerns.
  - Profile picture: As a teacher, you should carefully select an appropriate picture that you feel would impress your network friends. A formal studio portrait may represent your professional image, while a casual but professional picture could represent you as a professional teacher and still convey a certain personal touch. For example, you might choose a picture of yourself standing in front of a national

park sign to suggest that you are an outdoor person, or you might use a picture taken in your office with the computer as a background to represent your interest in technology integration. Photos that are too personal or too social are not appropriate for your professional identity.

- Similar rules can be applied to students. For younger students, consider not posting any face pictures, as this can lead to privacy and safety concerns. As an alternative, you can allow students to create their own avatars that represent their digital identity. Younger students enjoy creating these symbolic digital images.

TIPS

If avatars are to be used, give your students time to create their own avatar and upload them to their profile. Consider using the class time to allow each student the opportunity to present her avatar and explain its meaning and why it was chosen. Such activities can enhance students' self-awareness and result in more positive self-images and better digital social learning.

- Hobby/Interests: If you want your professional identities to have a personal touch, share your hobbies or interests in them.
- Photo albums: If you have photos that you would like to share with others, photo albums offer a great place to do this. For example, you could share photos of yourself giving a talk at a meeting or conference, receiving awards or honors, posing for professional group photos, and so on. For a more personal and social impression, you could share photos of a summer biking tour, national park trip, or museum visit to add a personal touch to your digital image. There are likely some photos that are more social or personal in nature, and you should avoid posting these on a social network profile intended for professional use. It is always important to ask yourself these questions: Do I want all of my social network friends to see these photos? Are they appropriate for all my network friends? If my network friends see these photos, what would they think about who I am?
- Social networking: SNSs generally contain features that allow you to connect with friends, fans, followers, or circles. Engage your students in social networking as a class or group. Urge them to only accept friend requests from people they know. This is particularly important with younger students. For more details, see chapter 4.
- Privacy setting: Most SNSs have privacy setting features. Read them carefully so you have a good understanding of the privacy policy. Encourage your students to read them carefully as well. For younger students, consider going through the privacy settings with them during class and discussing the importance of privacy settings with them.
- Update regularly: Update your profile regularly, based on your needs and situation, and encourage students to do the same. This step is as

important as the initial profile creation. Review your profile every semester, because you may need to update information, or you may want to reinvent your identity for a new class.

SUGGESTED ADDITIONAL ACTIVITY

Guess Who I Am

If time allows, engage students in an additional activity that gives them better knowledge and skills in developing their digital identities. This is also a good opportunity to evaluate your students' digital identities and to screen any inappropriate identities. Use these teaching moments to provide additional instructions for developing digital identities.

- Randomly project your students' digital profiles, and ask everyone to guess who they are. Consider removing identifiable pictures or photos from the profiles so the game won't be too easy for them.
- This activity can also be conducted as a team, with student teams competing to make the activity more fun.

Alternatively, print out all of your students' profiles and randomly distribute them to the students. Ask each student to present the profile he received, and allow the whole class to guess which profiles belong to which students.

TIPS

- Treat the digital profiles more like your own resume or curriculum vitae, and update the profile regularly.
- Remind students to update their profiles often to reflect their ideal digital identities.
- Always remember: If there is something you don't want people to know in a FTF setting, you do not want to share them online, either.
- Be responsible for your own digital profiles.

Case II:
Professional Personal Digital Social Identities

Developing digital identities by maintaining digital profiles involves an initial setup. Digital social identities include the shared social content and social communications occurring on SNSs that are recorded and become the digital social footprint. Generally, this type of communication is called "feeds" and is more like a person's face value. Anything you post and interact with in the live feed is potentially there forever. This is how people are going to remember who you are.

- Define your digital social identity: professional, social, or personal.
- Share social content
  - Share professional learning content and resources that you find online.
  - Share only carefully selected, relevant content with the social network groups you think could benefit from it.
  - Share reasonably with the right amount of resources. Avoid flooding your social network groups with a large amount of resources even if you think they are valuable to them. Oversaturating your feed with information and resources can clutter the feed, make the resources you share seem less important, and possibly annoy your connections and groups.
  - If you have a large amount of resources to share, consider dispersing them or sending them in smaller batches over time.
- Communicate
  - Respond to friends' shared content by using the "like" feature on Facebook, Retweet them on Twitter, or +1 for Google Circles.
  - Respond to these posts with your ideal digital social identity in mind. These responsive actions are seen as endorsing someone's thought, idea, or behavior, and therefore they can impact your digital social identity. For example, if you "like" a photo of your colleague drinking, your connections might perceive you as someone who also likes to drink.
  - Comment on friends' shared resources with your digital social identity in mind.
- Infuse a personal touch
  - If you would like to create your digital social identity with a personal touch, share or comment on shared resources with social or personal aspects.
  - Be cautious and use your best judgment on whether these social or personal touches are appropriate for different social network groups, particularly in teacher-student or professional network groups.

LAST WORDS

Social tagging resources can be seen on Delicious in chapter 1, Table 1.1.

What you say in face-to-face (FTF) settings may not be appropriate for all of your digital and digital social identities. This doesn't mean that you need to reduce or eliminate your online footprint. You simply need to organize, manage, and present it in a thoughtful and informed manner, just as you do in FTF settings. You want to impress different people with your different identities.

Educators and students should begin managing their digital identities as they would their physical identities by presenting to the public what they feel is their most desirable image; for example, wearing appropriate clothing for social presentation or speaking in a voice that conveys their communication in a style that is in keeping with their physical image. All of the presentations of self on participatory online sites constitute "simultaneously developing online identities, or dynamic and shifting constructions and presentations of self" (Coiro et al., 2008, p. 526). People are creative in producing their presumed best social images by sharing personal information, activities, pictures, videos, and so on to develop their desired self-presentation, and apply social networking technology to share remixed social media contents to mash-up collective expressions.

"Before you post something online, think about whether you would want your superior, a future employer or your family to see it. Even if the privacy settings are set correctly right now, you never know what might happen in the future that could expose old posts. This also goes for photos and videos. Any social content that you don't want the world to see should stay out of your online accounts" (Komando, 2012, para. 17). Once it's online, we have less control of it. So take the responsibility to manage it, just like celebrities. Think like a celebrity and act like a celebrity in the social networking world.

KEY LINKING THINKING

- What do I want different groups of people to know about me?
- I must manage my digital identity strategically and regularly.
- Should I share something that I don't normally share with others in the physical world? Probably not.
- All my online traces and activities are public and are online indefinitely—possibly forever.

CHAPTER 4

Learn to Be a Butterfly on Social Networks

Have you ever:

- Been intimidated by social network sites, such as Facebook or Twitter?
- Been invited by others to become their friends or to join their social network?
- Wondered what becoming a social network friend meant to your teaching or learning?
- Wondered how many social network friends you have, could have, or may need?

SOCIAL NETWORK DESIGN CONCEPTS

Social network linkage (SNL) refers to connecting to social networks by becoming friends, followers, or fans of others on Web 2.0 tools, thereby building tight social relationships, receiving updates on friends' learning activities and resources, and achieving social networking collaboration. Members of social networks are granted privileges to view more of their friends' resources and their social networks. By viewing the networks of friends, you can identify other people who have the same or similar interests to expand your learning network.

Many Web 2.0 tools provide a feature that allows you to connect to multiple people and networks. On Facebook, this is accomplished by adding a person as a "friend." On LinkedIn, you can connect to people through your professional or personal affiliation to them (i.e., colleague, friend, classmate, etc.). On Twitter, you can "follow" someone. By making a connection ("friend"), you can view that friend's learning resources via network feeds without visiting the friend's actual social network sites. With SNL, learners can share social content with specific friends rather than in an open network environment. This affords learners a more context-specific learning environment. With these features and SNL, you, as an educator, can engage learners and community members to share social content and to collaborate to achieve communities of practice and communities of inquiry.

When thinking about social networks, many consider Facebook or Twitter only. In SNL design, social network has a broader meaning. It refers to any site that uses social networking mechanisms to connect people in various ways, such as becoming friends, fans, followers, or circle members in order to share, view, and collaborate at more and deeper levels. Many Web 2.0 tools have embedded social networking features that allow the users to share, view, and collaborate more effectively. Examples of using social networking range from students following a course on Twitter for updates on course announcements to Delicious's following feature to share and to collaborate on social bookmarks.

Social media is not social until it is integrated with social network linkage design. Joining social media doesn't automatically achieve social collaboration. In other words, if you integrate Twitter into network instructions without asking learners to follow others, there is no social network, because no social network linkage has been established among learners and educators.

Social network linkage is important for providing outlets for informal, social, and unstructured learning (Selwyn, 2009). It helps learners feel socially connected, which is "a key factor in online course success and enables the development of group social structure and continued social interactions among individuals in an educational environment" (Slagter, van Tyron, and Bishop, 2009, p. 311). Jones et al. (2010) argue that students would like to use educational technology for learning because they need more communications platforms with peers and others, and they need peer sharing and encouragement. SNL allows "both educators and students to have more context-specific connection and communication with each other, or with people outside the classroom" (Jones et al., 2010, p. 779); and it provides a flexible environment for learner participation. This type of instruction "strengthens social learning context and provides a seamless user experience for learning and collaboration both formally and informally" (Ganiz, 2009, para. 27).

SOCIAL NETWORK DESIGN GUIDELINES

To Select the Tools with Social Network Features

There are two types of tools that can be integrated with SNL design: social network sites, such as Facebook, Twitter, or Google+; and Web 2.0 tools that have social network features, such as Delicious, Diigo, and Blogger.

Most people are aware of social network sites such as Facebook and Twitter, but they are not aware of Web 2.0 tools with social network features. It is obvious that SNSs are for social networking purposes. With non-SNS Web 2.0 tools, you need to determine whether the selected tools have social networking features, such as becoming friends, fans, or followers. Generally, Web 2.0 tools require users to create an account to access the tools; therefore, learners can use their own personal account to social network to create a learning group, working team, or circle. Do not overlook the social networking features in other Web 2.0 sites. Here are a few tools that have social networking features embedded:

- Delicious: Following
- Diigo: Following
- Blogger: Followers
- Google apps: Friends
- WordPress blog: Friends
- VoiceThread: Friends
- Skype: Contacts

To Organize a Social Network

After selecting the tools and creating tool accounts, be sure to ask your students to socially network with other learners to create a group, a working team, or a network community to share and collaborate on learning activities. To participate in a social network, most tools require the users to request to become friends and wait until the other party approves the friend request; but some tools require simply adding others as friends or following others without permission. For example, on Twitter, one can follow another by simply clicking the "Follow" button without requesting following permission. Check each tool for the details on how you can connect.

Some tools have additional social networking features for creating or forming a group or a community. Examples of this include Facebook groups, Facebook pages, Diigo groups, and Google Circles. These social network group features offer the groups the option to be in open or closed environments. Some groups are completely open, while some groups are open to members only, and some are in between. If your class requires more specific collaboration, consider using the social networking feature of Web 2.0 tools. This will allow the group members to share and to collaborate in a more organized fashion. For example, a course can create a course Facebook page for the students to collaborate on, share, and communicate any course learning instructions and resources. After creating a course Facebook page, students "like" the course page; this allows them to view and post any message onto the page. If needed, a course Facebook page can be integrated as a course discussion platform. Because students can "like" the course page, they can read and post the messages on their Facebook feeds without visiting the course Facebook page. This creates a more seamless collaboration.

To Share and Collaborate on Social Networks

After they sign up for social networking as friends or social network groups, encourage your students to actively communicate with their friends by sharing and collaborating on their learning resources.

To Link Tools to Social Network

Some Web 2.0 tools have additional non–social networking features that can enhance social networking activities. These include Google Circle linked to Google apps such as Google Calendar, Google Docs, Google Sites, and Google Groups. For example, within Google Circle, members can link their membership to Google Apps to make their social network sharing and collaborating easier and more effective.

Linking social network to mobile apps on mobile devices is another SNL feature design not to be overlooked. Many mobile apps have social networking features with location-based technology to enhance social network linkage in a more geo-location and context specific. The mobile apps include Foursquare, Facebook, SCVNGR, and Gowalla. These mobile apps are not essential to social networking functions, but they all have social networking features enhanced by location-based technology. By becoming friends via these mobile apps, users can see the location where their friends have checked in. These linkage designs can be particularly effective in conducting scavenger hunts, field studies, and other instructional activities. Linking social networks with location-based technology amplifies open network learning environments with physical environments.

SOCIAL NETWORK DESIGNS

To Create SNL Activities

- Encourage your students to join a social network with other students, teachers, or the courses by becoming friends, fans, or followers at the beginning of the instructions.
- Ask students to follow the course on Twitter, so they can receive course announcements via their Twitter account. If students have mobile devices, course announcements on Twitter can also be viewed on the mobile devices (see Learning Activity in this chapter).
- Direct students to form social network groups using Web 2.0 tools, so they can communicate, share, and collaborate on learning

resources more effectively and efficiently in the beginning of the instructions.

- Encourage students to join the course Diigo group, so they can share their social bookmarks on Diigo and share their social annotations with other students.
- Combine mobile social network tools with location-based technology to create learning activities to enhance both ONLE and physical environments.

SOCIAL NETWORK LINKAGE DESIGNS

We will use each linkage model to guide and inspire us to design effective SNL activities. It is not necessary for you to integrate all possible linkages from the linkage design model; but think through all possibilities to determine which linkages could be effective in your instruction. Then you can select those that are more relevant to your teaching.

Here are a few suggestions for applying each linkage to enhance your SNL instructions.

- *Personal portal linkage*: Encourage students to add SNL tools, such as Facebook, Twitter, and Google+, to their PLE. Suggest that they share their iGoogle gadgets with their friends.
- *RSS linkage*: Encourage students to use RSS feeds to receive updates on their friends' shared resources. This way, they do not need to visit each friend's feed to view the friend's shared resources. Instead, they can simply view their own social network feeds to view all friends' resource feeds.
- *Widget linkage*: Embed SNL widgets, such as instructional wiki pages on Facebook, Twitter, Google+, to web pages, so students can view SNL on instructional web pages without visiting multiple social network sites.
- *Social tagging linkage*: Most social network sites have social tagging features, which allow you to organize content and to collaborate with others. See the chapter resources for the social tagging instructions for Facebook, Twitter (hashtag), and LinkedIn.
- *Mobile linkage*: Encourage students to add SNL apps to their mobile devices. Integrate location-based technology on mobile devices to enhance SNL for mobile learning.
- *InfoViz linkage*: Use, and encourage students to use, InfoViz tools to assist in visualizing how their social network friends are connected and interconnected. With InfoViz, you can observe different groups of friends and their relationships. Some examples of InfoViz tools for social network friends are Facebook FriendWheel, Facebook TouchGraph, and Mentionmapp for Twitter.

LEARNING ACTIVITY:
SOCIAL CONTENT SHARING AND COLLABORATION

Purpose: Apply social network linkage design to support social content sharing and collaboration.

Instructions: There are four different cases that will introduce you to ways you can enhance your network instructions, by integrating social network in Twitter, Diigo, Delicious, and Foursquare with mobile devices.

Case I:
Instructional Announcements on Twitter

Typical network learning requires students to visit course instruction sites to review course announcements on course websites to course LMS, such as BlackBoardLearn. By integrating Twitter for instruction announcements, students can visit their Twitter account on Twitter, iGoogle, or mobile devices for the announcements, without visiting the instruction sites. Instructors can post instruction announcements by tweeting anytime and anywhere from a computer and any mobile device. Here is how to set up course announcements on Twitter.

- Obtain a course or an instruction Twitter account. Do not use your own Twitter account for either. This is particularly critical if you use your Twitter account for personal communication.
- Be sure to set up the instruction Twitter account as professional by configuring the "Profile."
- Set up "Close" or "Open" feature for the Twitter account
  - If you prefer the course Twitter in open network, be sure to uncheck Tweet Privacy under Profile Account setting. In this case, you do not need to approve requests to follow the course Twitter. Anyone can see the course tweets.
  - If you prefer a closed network, check Tweet Privacy. In this case, you must approve everyone who requests to follow the course Twitter, or they won't see the course tweets.

TIPS

For maximum effective management, uncheck Tweet Privacy at the beginning of the course, so you do not need to approve every student's request to follow the course on Twitter. After all students have signed up to follow the course Twitter, check Tweet Privacy to protect your course announcements.

REMINDER

Even if your students are familiar with Twitter, you should still spend time explaining how it works and how you will use course announcement with Twitter. Design some simple exercises, such as the following examples, to ensure that students have good understanding and the right expectations.

- Require students to follow the course Twitter, so they can see the course announcements without visiting the course Twitter site. Students can simply view the course announcement tweets on their Twitter site, iGoogle page, or Twitter apps on mobile devices. Establishing this social network linkage and following the course Twitter is crucial; otherwise, students need to visit the course Twitter site to get updated. This is particularly effective when students are engaged in multiple course announcements on Twitter. Students can view their Twitter sites to get updated on all the courses' announcement tweets.
- If you like, require student groups to follow their group members, so when they tweet, their group members can see their tweets.
- Expand SNL for Twitter by asking student groups to share and to collaborate by adding students to a "List." This is particularly useful if you like to assign students to collaborative groups, semesters, sessions, topics, and themes. For details, see the tutorials at http://delicious.com/chihtu/SONLE+SNL+Twitter.
- After setting up the course Twitter and SNL for students to follow, you are ready to tweet about your course announcements.
- To be sure students accept and fully understand this new integration, consider designing some simple exercises to engage them. Below are a few simple exercises:
  - In the beginning of the instructions, you can tweet a simple question and ask for students' response. Student who reply may receive extra points or other positive reinforcements
  - You can tweet useful online resources to support the instruction; ask the students to "retweet" it to others.
  - If you would like all students to see each other's tweets, integrate social tagging architecture by adding a course hashtag to the tweets. See chapter 11 for more information.

Case II:
Social Annotation Sharing and Collaboration on Diigo Group

As an instructor, you probably often assign students online reading, which they read and take notes on. These notes and annotations generally are personal rather than shared. Diigo, a social bookmarking site, allows users to bookmark, tag webpages, highlight online texts, and attach sticky notes to specific high-lights or to a whole page. By integrating this social network linkage into their PLEs, students can share and collaborate on their bookmarks and annotations in a closer context, Diigo Group. Here is how you set up a Diigo group.

- As an instructor, create a personal Diigo account. With Diigo, it is appropriate to create your own account. Under the umbrella of your account, you can create a course group.
- Create a Diigo group. Be sure to configure the access privilege for the group.
  - Who can view? Public vs. Private.
  - How to join? Apply to join. Moderator approval required vs. by invitation only.
  - Who can invite new members? Only group moderator vs. all group members.

Below are a few suggested activities for Diigo groups.

- Group members can share their online bookmarks with other group members.
- Instructor can assign online reading. Students read online and use the highlight feature to highlight the online content and attach comments, annotations to the highlighted area, or provide comments and annota-tions to the entire page.
- Turn the highlighted area or specific areas of the reading page into an online discussion thread. This type of discussion provides more context for learning since the discussion actually occurs on the reading rather than in an online discussion board.

LAST WORDS

Social tagging resources can be seen on Delicious in chapter 1, Table 1.1.
Social networks have earned a negative perception in the field of education. Social networking is frequently seen as abandoning physical social relationships, or becoming an "online social butterfly." With social network linkage design for learning, social networks can provide effective ways to enhance network collabo-ration in more secure and context-specific learning environments. ONLE doesn't mean everything has to be open. In fact, ONLE gives you a wider range of learn-ing environments in which to engage students. Based on the learners and your instructional needs, you can integrate social network linkage with a great deal of flexibility to design from more personal, social, or closed, to open environments.

KEY LINKING THINKING

- Does the tool need to have social networking features to integrate?
- How can I integrate social network linkage to improve network col-laboration?

PART III

NETWORK DIMENSION

Part III presents open and network learning architectures to connect tools, humans, and environments.

CHAPTER 5

Accrue RSS Linkage

Have you ever:

- Been overwhelmed by the large network of learning content?
- Visited multiple websites to view their online content?
- Visited multiple websites and noticed there is nothing new to read?
- Not remembered what you read already?

RSS DESIGN CONCEPTS

If you are overwhelmed by the sheer number of online learning resources, RSS linkage design could be an effective way to manage your online distributed learning resources. In this chapter, you will learn how to integrate RSS and RSS linkage to manage, organize, and share network content in ONLE.

RSS linkage refers to the linking application of an RSS feed from one site or tool to others, so learners can monitor learning content in one place and get updates on all live news feeds. RSS (RDF site summary, rich site summary, or really simple syndication) is simple XML (extensible markup language) syntax for identifying recent additions of content to a website. It allows online learners to subscribe independently to their choice of sources for content across the web. RSS thereby reduces the need for learners to visit many individual websites.

Many Web 2.0 tools—blogs, Twitter, wiki, YouTube, Google Calendar, Delicious—are equipped with RSS features. "RSS feeds became widespread with the advent and increasing use of blogs, and are currently one of the most important RSS applications. Generally, when a blogger adds a new entry, the blog's RSS feed will automatically" (Wu and Li, 2007, p. 39) inform every-one subscribing to the blog. However, these mechanisms are not limited to blogs only. Many Web 2.0 tools have embedded the RSS feed feature.

RSS linkage design offers network learners opportunities for learning social content, publishing, sharing, and collaborating. RSS linkage provides many advantages to learners, instructors, and instructional designers. For example, learners can access new shared or published content without accessing the site where the content was published. In other words, network learners can be updated with new content within their PLE (e.g., iGoogle). Within each individual learner's PLE, they can configure and organize their RSS aggregators, manage and retrieve the subscribed RSS feeds on any topic or keyword. Instructors and learners can set up their own RSS feeds to pub-lish and share their subscribed learning resources, and collaborate with other learners in the digital communities.

RSS DESIGN GUIDELINES

RSS can be linked to three main "divisions": Resources, People, and Tools, as well as to eight ONLE linkage designs. RSS linkage's main linking function involves linking network resources via RSS feed subscriptions. However, it also includes linking to people and to tools. Linking to people in RSS linkages allows learners to share and to collaborate with their friends and other network learners via RSS feed subscriptions. RSS feeds can be linked from one Web 2.0 tool to others to connect different personal learn-ing environments. The summary of RSS linkage design below will help you understand the design guidelines.

To Select Network Resources with RSS Feeds

To integrate RSS into your instructions, you must first select network re-sources that have RSS feeds. Many websites or tools are embedded with RSS feeds. Visit the websites and look for the RSS icon (Figure 5.1). Gener-ally you can find the RSS icon on your Internet browser's URL field or on the web page. The RSS icon is generally clickable. The steps below will help guide you to identify and develop network resources with RSS feeds.

Figure 5.1   RSS Icon

- Check your existing integrated web re-sources or websites for RSS feed availability. Many of them have RSS feeds.
- Generally, most wiki, blog, or library sites have RSS feeds.
- Subscribe to them via your RSS aggregator tool (e.g., Google Reader).

- Note: Generally, learning management systems (LMS), such as BlackBoard, do not have RSS features embedded, since they are closed systems. Check with your LMS for the availability of RSS.

If it is more effective to build your own web content and resources, you need to select the website/pages building tools that have the RSS feed feature, such as wiki and blogs. If your learning content and resources require a larger space on the webpage and a navigation menu to organize them, a wiki may be more effective. If the content and resources require constant posting and are viewed chronologically, a blog would be a more effective tool to publish your network resources.

To Organize RSS Feeds

For the retrieval of RSS feeds, RSS aggregators are needed. There are a number of RSS aggregators available online as well as downloadable client-based and browser-based applications, such as Google Reader, Internet browsers (Firefox, IE, Chrome, etc.), MS Outlook, and so on. They provide feeds related to blog updates, newspaper and journal articles, announcements, news and database updates.

RSS aggregators, such as Google Reader, allow learners to track and organize the information they receive by category. Learners make an active decision to access information rather than having it presented directly to them. They have a chance to select, organize, and manage preferred RSS feeds as part of PLE. In this sense, RSS linkage design is related to constructivism. It is because of this relationship that Siemens (2007) states learning is a network forming and connecting process with critical decision making.

Which RSS aggregator to integrate? Ideally, you should allow learners to select their own RSS aggregators based on their own preferences, which result in a better design for individual learning. If your learners are less experienced in RSS, you may want to consider requiring them to use the same RSS aggregator, but encourage them to explore other aggregators as well. The most valuable part of ONLE is that learners can personalize their environments by selecting their own preferred tools rather than the ones required or provided by the educators. Although using different tools, learners and educators are still able to share and collaborate in learning activities. The best design allows each learner to select his or her preferred learning tools that have RSS mechanisms. Although tools are personalized but have common RSS mechanisms, different selected tools can connect and communicate with one another, and communicate with other learners' selected tools.

REMINDER

The mechanisms of RSS are relatively new to most learners. If you intend to integrate RSS to network your learning resources, be sure to provide instructions to help your learners understand how RSS and RSS feeds/subscriptions work. Additionally, consider explaining the value of RSS linkage and integration.

To Share RSS Feeds and Collaborate with Others

ONLE without social sharing and social collaboration would not be effective. Although RSS is a network mechanism orientated to resources, a human social network is still the key to effective learning. As an educator, you need to add social sharing and collaboration to RSS linkage. RSS feeds may not have social sharing and collaboration embedded; however, some RSS aggregators have sharing and collaboration features that can be integrated to support RSS feed sharing and collaboration. E-mailing the feeds or transmitting them by other means can also accomplish sharing and collaborating in RSS feeds.

To Link Tools to RSS

RSS feeds can be integrated with other Web 2.0 tools, such as iGoogle, wiki, blog, Diigo, Delicious, Google Calendar, network discussion board, Internet browser, e-mail applications, mobile devices, and Dipity. In linking different tools together, RSS functions as a mechanism that connects multiple tools together, and organizes and centralizes learning resources and activities into one web location. This is particularly critical when you integrate multiple Web 2.0 tools to support your instruction. For example, you may integrate a wiki and a blog into the instruction, which would require learners to visit the wiki and blog in two separate web locations. A more effective design would be to embed a blog's RSS feeds onto the wiki pages. With this design, learners can visit a wiki site and view both wiki and blog instructional resources. Similar tool linking can be applied by using RSS linkage to display Delicious or Diigo's social tagging resources on wiki pages.

RSS ACTIVITY DESIGNS

To Create RSS Activities

Simply selecting and creating RSS feed content doesn't guarantee that learners will be engaged in interactive learning. In order to accomplish that, you need to create and design RSS activities to engage learners in learning. Below are a few suggested activities to engage learners in RSS.

- To engage the students in using an RSS aggregator, use multiple RSS feeds for your instructions, and be sure to require the learners to subscribe to them.
- Ask students to subscribe to course instructions, contents, and resources that have RSS features.
- If learners are new to RSS, you could provide and collect the RSS feeds and display them on one page, such as on wiki, and require the learners to subscribe. If the learners are more experienced in RSS feeds, you can just provide instructions to subscribe to the required RSS feeds.
- To encourage network collaboration, consider asking students to share their RSS feed subscriptions with you, with their collaborative groups, or with the whole class. This way, the collective RSS feed subscriptions become living network learning resources. This is particularly valuable with students new to the class, because this design engages community-community interaction between current and previous students.
- If you integrate PLE, such as iGoogle, into your ONLE instructions, consider asking students to add an RSS gadget to their iGoogle. That way, learners can monitor and organize their RSS feeds in one central location on their PLE.

LINKAGE DESIGNS FOR RSS

Besides connecting to three dimensions—tools, people, and resources—the linkage design model can also be used to assist in designing more effective and comprehensive ONLE. You can use each linkage model as a guide and to inspire you to design effective RSS activities. It is not necessary to integrate all linkages from the linkage design model, but consider all linkages to see whether any of them could make your instruction more effective. Then select those that are more relevant to your teaching and instructions.

Here are a few suggestions for applying linkages to enhance your RSS instructions.

- *Personal portal linkage*: Encourage students to add an RSS gadget to iGoogle or to other personal portal tools; that way, they can manage their RSS subscriptions in one central location.
- *Widget linkage*: Many websites, such as wiki, offer gadgets that allow you to embed RSS feeds to display current content from the feed by widget linkage design.
- *Social tagging linkage*: Some RSS aggregators, such as Google Reader, have social tagging features that allow students to apply tags to organize and share their RSS feed subscriptions. If you use a "social tagging architecture" (see chapter 11) for your instructions, remember

to apply it to RSS feeds, so your students know which tags to use to organize and share their RSS feeds.

- *Social network linkage*: Some RSS aggregators allow learners to become friends/fans and to share and collaborate via their RSS feeds. Students can become friends or fans as a class or group to streamline sharing and collaboration and make it more private. Within a class or a collaborative group within the class, learners can share their RSS feeds with others in a more private or semi-open environment, rather than sharing everything in public.

- *Mobile linkage*: Many mobile devices have apps for RSS feeds. If your learners have access to any mobile devices, such as smart-phones or tablet computers, ask students to download RSS apps so they can view their RSS feed subscriptions on these devices. If not all of your students have access to mobile devices, encourage them to apply RSS apps to support their RSS feeds. Which mobile RSS apps should students use? Let them select their own. Additionally, you can encourage them to rate and share their favorite mobile apps with the class, to help others to select the right mobile app in the future.

- *InfoViz linkage*: Some RSS aggregators have features that do more than just organize RSS feeds. For example, Google Reader has an analytic feature that analyzes RSS feed subscription usages and displays them in statistical charts (last 30 days, time of day, day of the week), tag clouds, subscription trends (frequently updated, inactive, and most obscure), and reading trends (read, clicked, starred, emailed, and mobile). Additionally, based on your RSS usage, Google Reader will suggest other RSS items and feeds with relevant learning content for you to access. In combining Google Reader's analytics and InfoViz linkage, you empower learners to manage, organize, and analyze their learning resources. Because students take full control of their PLE, they are encouraged to set up their own learning goals, monitor their learning progress, and adjust progress based on the InfoViz on their RSS feed learning activities.

LEARNING ACTIVITY:
MULTIPLE RSS LINKAGE DESIGN FOR INSTRUCTION TIMELINE

Purpose: To centralize all course instructional activities and display them in a timeline-based format of Information Visualization (InfoViz), thereby enabling learners and instructors to visualize and monitor instructional activities in one central timeline figure. See the example at http://www.dipity.com/chihhsiungtu/Dr-Tus-Course-Timeline/.

Table 5.1 Multiple Web 2.0 Tools for the Course Instructions

Course instructions	Delivery tools
Course website	Wetpaint wiki
Course announcement	Twitter
Course calendar	Google Calendar
Course resources	Delicious
Course blog	Blogger
Course activity timeline	Dipity

In this Learning Activity, multiple Web 2.0 tools are employed to deliver the course instructions. See Table 5.1.

All of these tools have an RSS feed feature. Dipity (http://www.dipity.com/), a digital timeline tool, is used to organize course instructional activities by date and time. Students can create their own interactive and visually enhancing timelines by integrating multimedia contents (video, audio, images, and texts), hyperlinks, social media content, geo-location information, time stamps, and RSS feeds. These created timelines can be strategically shared, embedded, and collaborated on with other network learners and digital citizens. The timeline applies a dynamic information visualization feature to display photos, videos, news, and RSS content in chronological order. Learners and instructors can monitor instructional activities and content in a visual chronological format.

- If you don't have any existing instructions on Web 2.0 tools for students, create them.
- Obtain the RSS feed URL from each Web 2.0 tool that you integrate.
- Obtain a Dipity account at http://www.dipity.com/.
- Create a "topic" to display your course instruction timeline.
- Input each RSS feed URL into your Dipity topic.
- Use embedded code to embed the timeline as a widget (widget linkage) back to your instructional wiki site or other website that you prefer.

As you can see in this learning activity, it is not necessary to use a lot of Web 2.0 tools to deliver your instructions. However, even if you have one RSS feed, you can display it in Dipity. Dipity has multiple display formats besides timeline (e.g., flipbook, list, map). Decide which display format is most appropriate for your instructions and for your students. After linking your RSS feeds to your Dipity topic, your Dipity topic will display your instruction activities live. Whenever there is a new feed content added to your instructions, it will be displayed on your Dipity timeline.

Social tagging resources can be seen on Delicious in chapter 1, Table 1.1.

CHAPTER 6

Believe in the Wonder of Widgets

Have you ever:

- Been required to visit multiple websites to view the resources?
- Thought of bringing different web resources into one central location to share with your students?

WIDGET LINKAGE DESIGN CONCEPTS

Widget linkages refer to stand-alone applications that can be embedded into third-party sites by students or instructors on a page where they have rights of authorship (e.g., a webpage, blog, or profile on a social media site). Widget linkages refer to linking mechanisms that allow students or instructors to insert or embed a stand-alone application or object into a third-party website where they have the privilege of creating or editing website content, such as HTML webpages, blog, wiki pages, or profile on social networking sites. This linkage empowers users to access social network resources based on their preferences rather than by visiting each tool site. By integrating this linkage, students and instructors can connect people, resources, and tools in their PLE. Educators can provide access to information by selecting and embedding different widgets into their instructional webpages, such as video, other webpages, survey, voting, clock, calendar, weather, calculator, and news. This allows students to access resources easily and quickly in more personalized formats. Learners have opportunities to manage their PLEs.

Educators generally integrate more than one Web 2.0 tool to support their instruction. Without linkage, even integrating two tools requires both students and teachers to visit each tool separately. Widget linkages allow students to access learning instructions from multiple Web 2.0 tools without having to visit each tool individually. For example, a course wiki containing course content can be composed of widgets fed from multiple tools such as other webpages, Google Calendar, YouTube, Diigo, RSS, Delicious, and Twitter. In other words, a course wiki mash-up with aggregate network resources can be displayed on a central website or webpage. The resources in the widgets generally are live feeds or real-time information; therefore, if the original sites update the information, the information and resources in the widgets are updated immediately as well. Most Web 2.0 tools have features that allow users to obtain widgets and embed them in other webpages without requiring special technical skills. Frequently, users need simply to copy and paste the codes or scripts.

WIDGET LINKAGE DESIGN GUIDELINES

To Select Tools and Widgets

Generally, widgets are linked to websites or webpages, such as regular webpages or wiki pages. The first step in creating a widget linkage is to select a website or webpage as your central online instruction page. Then you can apply widget linkage design to connect other tools to your wiki pages. Most wiki tools, such as Google Sites, Wikispaces, and Wetpaint, are compatible with widget technology. On the other hand, be sure the Web 2.0 tools that you intend to link to your wiki have widget features. Some tools may refer to widgets as Google apps widgets, or embedded scripts. Some Web 2.0 tools have more than one widget available for different functions. You can embed all widgets to your webpages or select only the ones relevant to your instructions.

To Organize Widgets

Any webpage allows you to embed as many widgets as you like. Instructors can organize the embedded widgets according to their instructional needs. To better organize these embedded widgets, you need to list the source under each widget, so the students know it is an embedded widget and where to find the source. This is also critical in regard to complying with copyright law.

To Share and Collaborate on Widgets

Widgets are portable and shareable to most webpages; therefore, they can be shared easily with network friends. You can do this simply by distributing the widget links or the embedded source code. Frequently, a simple copy and paste can be applied for sharing and collaborating.

To Link Tools to Widgets

A widget itself is a node that links two web tools or webpages. The selected tools and webpages that are linked must be compatible with widget technology. Certain LMS, such as BlackBoardLearn, may not be compatible with widgets, while others, such as Moodle, are compatible and easily embedded. Before applying widgets to link your tools and webpages, check with the tools or software administrators or the technical support people in your institution to see if the tools or webpages you intend to link are compatible with widget linkage design.

WIDGET LINKAGE ACTIVITY DESIGNS

To Create Widget Activities

- Create your online instructions on a wiki by integrating widget linkage design to aggregate and mash up network learning resources.
- Have students collaborate on assignments on a wiki by incorporating widget linkage to aggregate and mash up network learning resources (see the Learning Activity in this chapter).
- Create PLE by applying widget linkage design to aggregate and mash up network learning resources (see chapter 6).

WIDGET LINKAGE DESIGNS

You can use each linkage model to guide and inspire you to design effective widget linkages. It is not necessary to integrate all linkages from the linkage design model, but carefully consider all linkages to see which ones would be most effective in your instructions. Then select those that are most relevant to your teaching and instructions.

Below are a few suggestions on how to apply each linkage to enhance your RSS instructions.

- *Personal portal linkage*: iGoogle is a perfect example of widget linkage design. Students and teachers can create a wiki site as their own personal learning portal by embedding multiple widgets to their wiki site. That way, students and teachers can view their own wiki sites as their PLE to monitor, manage, and organize their learning resources.
- *RSS linkage*: Typical wiki sites have widget features for adding any RSS feed to the site, so your wiki site is able to display the live feed resources.
- *Social network linkage*: Widgets are portable and shareable with your network friends or others. Generally, widgets can be shared by copying and pasting a link or embedded source code. iGoogle's

gadget sharing is a good example of social network linkage (see chapter 4). Generally, the sharing feature is delivered via e-mail.

- *Mobile linkage*: Widgets work like mobile apps. They are portable and shareable. Check the Web 2.0 tools you integrate to see if they have mobile apps available for mobile devices. For example, Facebook, Twitter, YouTube, VoiceThread, and RSS have both widgets and mobile apps available to enhance your linkage design.

LEARNING ACTIVITY: AGGREGATE LEARNING CONTENT

Purpose: To integrate widget linkage design and enrich network learning content and resources for educators and students.

Instructions: In these two case studies, teachers and students integrate widget linkage design to aggregate and mash up network learning resources as learning content.

Case I:
Aggregate Course Learning Instructions for Teachers

Regardless of whether the instruction is FTF or online, it is inevitable that teachers need to create and integrate online learning resources to enhance their instructions. In this case, you will use a wiki to create and aggregate online resources for your online instructions.

- Select a wiki tool, such as Google Sites, Wikispaces, or Wetpaint.
- Create and develop the learning content that is specific for your instruction. If the content or resources can be found online, consider applying widget linkage to display them dynamically on your wiki pages.
- Add the widgets from the selected Web 2.0 tools. If you integrate other Web 2.0 tools to support your instructions, such as Facebook, Twitter, YouTube videos, calendars, or RSS feeds, check the availability of widgets for each tool.
- Copy and paste the link or embedded source codes to your wiki pages by following the wiki tool's instructions for inserting a widget.
- Embed webpages in your wiki pages. Copy and paste the webpage URL, and insert the URL by following the wiki instructions for inserting a webpage.
- Check that the widget displays correctly, so that it presents live feeds or information clearly.
- Place the source name and URL below the widget, to abide by copyright law.

Case II:
Learner-Generated eTextbooks

Creating and developing online learning content and resources is fairly easy technically. In this Learning Activity, you will lead students in creating learner-generated chapters for a textbook. This activity engages students in real-world and meaningful instructional activities.

- Design your textbook outline. As a teacher, you should create the textbook outline that you would like your students to develop. How detailed you should be depends on your students' level of knowledge and technical skills in the content area.
- Divide students into groups. Since developing textbook chapters is time-consuming, it is more efficient to do this activity as a group task. Each group can be responsible for at least one chapter.
- Explain the purpose of learner-generated textbooks. Explain to the students that their tasks are to create a textbook chapter for classmates or future students to study on a certain topic. Let them know that their chapters will be assembled as a textbook for future students to study.
- Design clear guidelines, criteria, and evaluation methods to allow the groups to follow. (Example: https://sites.google.com/site/etc 655/chapter-rubrics.)
- Select a wiki tool that allows the groups to create and develop their chapter content collaboratively.
- Require the group to create certain content and allow them to aggregate online learning content and resources.

Demonstrate how to integrate widget linkage design to aggregate the chapter's learning content (see Case I for inserting widgets and webpage to wiki pages). Allow ample time to accomplish this task.

- Ask the group to cite widget sources for each embedded widget.
- Assemble all chapters into the textbook.
  - Convert each chapter on wiki to a PDF document, and combine all chapters into a textbook as a single PDF.
  - Use Apple's iBook Author, or other free book-publishing tool, to assemble all book chapters. (For iBook Author instructions, see http://www.educatorstechnology.com/2012/11/great-video-tutorials-on-creating.html.) By using iBook Author to create textbooks, authors can still own the copyright. For more information, see http://support.apple.com/kb/HT5071#3
  - Assemble the textbook (see Delicious link).
- Provide credits in the book or the website that contains the textbook information for all students who participate in the textbook project. Encourage students to announce their textbook project on their social network sites, such as Facebook, Twitter, or blogs.

- Upload the textbook to the course wiki site or any wiki sites, or Google Sites. Allow students to download the eTextbook.
- Share the eTextbook with other classes through course Twitter announcements, blogs, Facebook page/group, outside of the school, or in a global community, if all students agree to share publically.

SUPPLEMENT ACTIVITIES

If you continue this eTextbook project every semester, each semester will generate a new edition of the textbook. After multiple semesters, your class will have multiple editions of it. Here are additional instructional activities that you can integrate to enrich learning interaction and collaboration.

- Ask upcoming students to read the eTextbooks created by previous students.
- Ask students to evaluate each chapter or the whole eTextbook with different editions. Tell them they are acting as reviewers and that they should read and write a book review that helps them develop their own book chapter.
- Provide a rating scheme (e.g., 1–10 or 1–5 stars). Students can rate each chapter or the whole eTextbook.

Allow student groups to aggregate the previous eTextbook resources into their book chapters by social tagging the chapters in eTextbooks on social tagging sites, such as Delicious or Diigo.

LAST WORDS

Social tagging resources can be seen on Delicious in chapter 1, Table 1.1.

When using wiki technology, creating online learning content is just like using a word processor; when employing widget linkage, developing online learning content and resources is just using drag and drop. Developing rich and comprehensive online learning instructions is no longer a challenging task. Educators and students can apply widget features, offered by most Web 2.0 tools, to develop and aggregate online learning resources. So keep linking one tool to another.

KEY LINKING THINKING

- Does the tool I'm using have a widget to link to my instructional webpages?
- What online learning resources can I aggregate into my instructional webpages by using widget linkage design?

CHAPTER 7

Discover the Hidden Power of Third-Party Linkage

Have you ever:

- Wondered whether and how you can make a single announcement to the students in all the courses you are teaching simultaneously?
- Been overwhelmed by multiple calendars to which you subscribe?
- Updated the same documents, calendar, or resources multiple times because they reside in multiple locations?

THIRD-PARTY LINKAGE DESIGN CONCEPTS

Third-party linkage refers to the application of third-party tools to link multiple Web 2.0 tools so news feeds can be streamed from one tool to other tools. It is not uncommon to have multiple channels of resources to organize and manage with the integration of multiple Web 2.0 tools. For example, you may have multiple calendars to consolidate, such as personal calendars, school calendars, and class calendars. Or you might have some resources you would like to share within different tools to reach different social network groups. Traditionally, you would need to visit each individual tool or site to view and manage these resources. Third-party linkage design allows you to centralize these scattered tools and functions into one tool so all tools and sites synchronize via cloud computing technology. You can visit one tool, site, or device to view and manage multiple channels of resources.

The third-party tools that you can use to accomplish this include Google Sync, Google Cloud Connect for MS Office, If This Then That (IFTTT), RSS mechanism, and Patchlife. Google Sync allows you to synchronize e-mails, calendars, and contacts from different accounts or sites. Google

Cloud Connect allows users to synchronize their MS Office documents, spreadsheets, and slides with Google Docs so users can access their MS Office files from Google Docs. IFTTT is a service that allows learners to create connections among different channels. Each individual channel contains unique triggers and actions. Twitter, e-mail, Facebook, Blogger, LinkedIn, RSS feeds, YouTube, and SkyDrive are examples of IFTTT channels. RSS is a Web 2.0 mechanism that is useful because most Web 2.0 tools are equipped with RSS features that function as a perfect third-party linkage to connect different tools. Patchlife is the online journal that gathers your digital memories and shows information in a stream about your past activities. Memolane, similar to Patchlife, allows users to connect different Web 2.0 tools and consolidate them into a horizontal timeline.

You may already use a course blog, Facebook page, or Twitter account to support your instruction. To update these pages with any new resources, you have to visit each tool individually, repeating your new additions in each. With Twitterfeed or IFTTT, a third-party tool that feeds your blog postings to Twitter, Facebook, and other tools, you can share a resource to the blog. The same resources will be fed simultaneously to Twitter, Facebook, and other social networking tools. With an additional e-mail to blog feature, you can use e-mail to post to your blog postings. This is particularly effective when your social network "friends" have their own preferred social network sites, which may be different than yours. Some are bloggers, some are active in Facebook, while others use Twitter. Regardless of their social network preferences, you can reach them and share resources strategically with third-party linkage design.

If you use Twitterfeed as a teaching tool, you and your students can e-mail message postings to the course blog without visiting the site; and these course blog postings are then fed to the course Facebook page and course Twitter, while tweets are fed to the course schedule, which is posted on a site such as Dipity (see chapter 12). The same messages can also be e-mailed to multiple course networks. The initial step is just a simple e-mail, so learners and instructors can even perform and access this linkage from smartphones.

You should also consider Posterous, a personal online sharing space as a third-party linkage, because it integrates an automatic posting to other social media tools such as Flickr, Twitter, and Facebook. Third-party linkages support you and your students and allow you to obtain better social network content management and organization. They eliminate all duplicate postings and tedious multiple tool usages.

THIRD-PARTY LINKAGE DESIGN GUIDELINES

To Select Network Resources to Be Linked

The first step of third-party linkage is to determine what type of resources you would like to use your third-party tool to link together. These resources can be blog feeds, Twitter feeds, Facebook feeds, calendars, bookmarks, e-mails, contacts, documents, and so on. After determining which resources to link, search for a third-party tool to use for linking. For a tool evaluation example, see Web 2.0 tool evaluation template: https://docs.google.com/document/d/1EfXcEx5XrQ5dVAkLJ1o6n6EKaGLbhrQwwi7HJ98QOeM/edit?usp=sharing.

Third-party tools are not as easy to find as Web 2.0 tools because generally they connect Web 2.0 tools and run in the background. An effective way to find third-party tools is to use an Internet search engine to search with right algorithm: "how to connect, link, or sync tool 1 with tool 2," for example, "how to connect blog to Twitter," or "how to sync Google Calendar with Outlook Calendar." After identifying a third-party tool, use the criteria listed below to evaluate different features offered by the third-party tool.

- What Web 2.0 tools does it connect? Some third-party tools may connect more than two Web 2.0 tools. The more tools it connects, the more flexible and effective it is.
- Is it available on multiple operation systems, Windows, Mac, Android, iOS, Linux?
- Is it easy to configure linking setting? Some tools may require a certain level of programming knowledge, while others are user-friendly.
- Is it available on an Internet browser, or does it require downloading and installing on a computer? Certainly, a browser-based third-party tool is more useful since it can be accessed from anywhere and at any time. For example, Twitterfeeds is a browser-based third-party tool, while Google Sync requires downloading and installing on a local computer.
- Is it available on all platforms, desktop/laptop computers, mobile apps (tablets and smartphones)?
- Does it have a feature to embed the third-party tool onto another website? For example, Dipity is a digital timeline tool that gathers different feeds and displays them as a timeline format that can be embedded onto wiki pages, Google Sites pages, and HTML webpages.

To Organize Third-Party Linkage

Before your third-party tool can be effective, it must be configured to ensure that the resources are linked correctly. You can draw a simple flow-chart or map to assist you in understanding how your linkage works. By utilizing strategic planning and designs, third-party linkage designs can be fairly sophisticated. This is particularly useful when you integrate many

Web 2.0 tools. This chart or figure can be included in your own PLE or your course PLE (see chapter 8). See a third-party linkage design figure at https:// docs.google.com/open?id=0B02hmofyxKPkTEdGN0JpX2JuX28.

To Share and Collaborate on Third-Party Linkage

The purposes of third-party linkage design are to consolidate, share, and collaborate on multiple resources. With thoughtful planning, users can collaborate with others via third-party linkage and share the resources effortlessly. For example, you can collaborate with another teacher in sharing their teaching resources.

To Link Tools to Third-Party Linkage

The primary purpose of third-party linkage is to link tools. Third-party linkage tools are not easily found since there are not many available. For an optimal effect, it is critical that you keep learning about new linking tools. Besides the tools mentioned in this chapter, share any others that you find with other readers using the tags SONLE or 3rdParty. Keep asking yourself: is there a way to connect one tool to other tools? Examine each tool carefully. RSS probably is the most common third-party linking tool since it is typically available in most Web 2.0 tools. If the tools have RSS features, it is likely that you can link those tools to one another.

THIRD-PARTY LINKAGE ACTIVITY DESIGNS

To Create Third-Party Activities

- *For teachers*: Share and post course resources and announcements by e-mailing the resources to the course blog. Use Twitterfeed as a third-party tool to feed blog postings to your course Twitter, Facebook page, and other Web 2.0 tools.
- *For students*: Subscribe to the course calendar on Google Calendar, and use Google Sync to synchronize the course calendar with personal and work calendars.

THIRD-PARTY LINKAGE DESIGNS

Third-party linkage designs focus on linking tools and resources. Combining with other types of linkages can result in more thorough and sophisticated integration for instruction.

Below are a few suggestions for applying other linkages to enhance your third-party linkage designs.

- *RSS linkage*: The RSS mechanism is the main force for linking different Web 2.0 tools, because most have RSS features. When selecting Web 2.0 tools to support your instructions, be sure to determine whether the tool has an RSS feature. If yes, the tool would support RSS linkage and functions as a third-party linkage design.
- *Mobile linkage*: Although third-party tools mainly link and sync with computers, some, like Google Sync, link and sync with mobile devices as well.
- *InfoViz linkage*: By combining third-party and InfoViz linkage designs, you can create multiple modes for resource analysis. This is especially available through RSS linkage. For example, Twitterfeed allows tracking the RSS feeds in real time, while Dipity displays RSS feed activities in a visual timeline format to enrich the learning context.

LEARNING ACTIVITY:
STREAMLINE RESOURCE SHARING

Purpose: To share instructional resources with multiple tools in a simple process.

Instructions: In this Learning Activity, you will enable a third-party tool to share resources with multiple tools and centralize multiple calendars into Google Calendar.

Case I:
Streamline Resources Posting and Sharing

In this case, you will set up a third-party linkage so you can e-mail resources or course announcements to your course blog. By applying Twitterfeed, the course blog will feed the shared resources and announcements to the course Twitter and Facebook pages. Additionally, your course Twitter RSS feeds to Dipity and is displayed in a visual timeline format (this design is illustrated in chapter 12).

In this Learning Activity, you learn how to use multiple Web 2.0 tools to deliver the course instructions. (See Table 7.1.) Note: This case is an extension of the case introduced in chapter 5.

- Set up a Twitterfeed account and any other account you might choose to use. (You do not need to set up any account that is not required for your instructions. Only a Twitterfeed account is required. If Facebook page is integrated, your Facebook account is required.)
- Log into your Twitterfeed account.

Table 7.1   Apply a Third-Party Tool to Support Multiple Web 2.0 Integration

Course instructions	Delivery tools
Third-Party Tool	Twitterfeed
E-mail	Your e-mail account
Course announcement	Twitter
Course blog	Blogger
Course collaboration	Facebook page
Course activity timeline	Dipity

- Create new feed.
- Follow the screen prompt to complete the linkage.
- After linking Twitterfeed to Facebook or Twitter, be sure to e-mail a test message to the blog to make sure the posting is viable.

Case II:
Sync Multiple Calendars

If you have the calendar that resides on MS Outlook and other calendars that reside on Google Calendar or Google Sync, a third-party linkage tool allows you to consolidate all your calendars. This way, you do not need to visit different locations to view different calendars.

- Download Google Sync at http://dl.google.com/dl/googlecalendar sync/googlecalendarsync_installer.exe.
- Follow the screen prompt to complete the installation and configuration.
- For more instructions, please follow Google Sync's tutorial to complete the setup process.

LAST WORDS

Social tagging resources can be seen on Delicious in chapter 1, Table 1.1.

Third-party linkage is a hidden power. It is not easy to identity third-party linkage tools since there are not many available. By asking yourselves the key linking questions below, you can find the right third-party linkage tools. Examine them carefully. Please share the third-party tools that you find with other readers using the tags SONLE or 3rdParty.

KEY LINKING THINKING

- Is there a way to link one tool to another tool?
- Can I perform a function without visiting multiple tools to complete it?

PART IV

INTEGRATION DIMENSION

Part IV emphasizes social and collaborative community activities in ONLE instructional strategies.

CHAPTER 8

Construct Your PLE

Have you ever:

- Been overwhelmed by too much website information?
- Logged in to multiple accounts to access online information?
- Forgotten your online log-in information, such as username and password?
- Visited multiple e-mail accounts to review your e-mail?
- Visited multiple sites to get updated with the learning resources you need?
- Wished there were a single site where you could monitor and manage your e-mail, class/work calendars, news, blogs, social network sites such as Facebook and Twitter, weather, and other information?

PLE DESIGN CONCEPTS

If you are overwhelmed by visiting multiple websites and logging in to multiple web accounts, personal portal linkage design can be an effective way to manage your online distributed learning environment. In this chapter, you will learn how to integrate PLE tools to manage and monitor multiple Web 2.0 tools. The skills and knowledge for this linkage design are critical for students and teachers.

When instructors integrate Web 2.0 tools to support their teaching, inevitably they end up using multiple Web 2.0 tools, which means creating multiple Web 2.0 accounts, with multiple log-ins to these accounts, and visiting multiple sites. PLE tools, such as iGoogle and Netvibes, can assist educators (and students) in organizing and managing multiple Web 2.0 learning tools—all in one central location. Additionally, PLE tools can help you monitor each Web 2.0 tool without actually visiting each site.

Personal portal linkage is a customized portal technology that links multiple Web 2.0 tools in one central location, and allows instructors and students to manage their learning content, information, and communications. If you are integrating any of these tools—Twitter, Google Calendar, Gmail, Google Docs—it would be more effective to engage your learners by having them set up individual iGoogle accounts as their PLEs. PLE is a curation of media tools and services, "brought together under the conceptual notion of openness, interoperability, and learner control" (Siemens, 2007, para. 2). Ideal PLEs empower learners to set their learning goals, manage their learning content and process, and communicate and collaborate with others.

Integrating personal portal linkage design to support learners in creating their PLEs is critical. Greenhow, Robelia, and Hughes (2009) argue that Web 2.0 empowers learners and their interconnections through the affordances of learner-defined linkages, shared multimodal content, prominent personal profiling, and inter-technology applications. With affordances, digital-age learners are required to gain competent digital literacy, which includes knowing how and when to select and manage which technologies (Barron, 2006, p. 194) to support their learning and knowing which forms and functions are most appropriate for their purposes. Educators' responsibility is to understand "how to facilitate learners' capacity to construct coherent meanings from the changing array of people, artifacts, and impressions they encounter in their everyday lives" (Greenhow, Robelia, and Hughes, 2009, p. 250).

A PLE is "comprised of two elements, the tools and the conceptual notions that drive how and why learners select individual parts" (Siemens, 2007, para. 2). A PLE is a concept-entity and is different from a product like e-portfolio. Siemens (2007) argues that PLEs are ecologies that utilize media elements but in themselves are not media. They are a live space for a person to manage, organize, and reorganize social media. PLEs require users to have management and organization skills sufficient to expand their learning ability and capability. Brown (1999) explained the social nature of learning: "Learning becomes as much social as cognitive, as much concrete as abstract, and becomes intertwined with judgment and exploration."

PLEs provide a way to solve the fragmented learning offered by Web 2.0 technology, because they integrate tools and learning based on personal learning experiences and personal learning style and selected tools. Make sure your students understand the importance of the conceptual notion of PLEs' creation and management. Effective PLEs should go beyond a single instruction, course, or activity. They can be extended to support personal learning outside of the classroom, work and career, and entertainment purposes. It is critical that each student builds a PLE at the start of their learning and continue on with it, throughout life. Learners in Web 2.0 PLEs are required to self-regulate learning skills to manage multiple learning tools because "self-regulated learning is predicated on the assumption that individuals can act as causal agents in their own learning process and environment" (Barnard-Brak, Lan, and Paton, 2010, para. 4). As such, "agency is the capability of individual human beings to make choices and to act on these choices in ways that make a difference in their lives" (Martin, 2004, p. 135).

PLE DESIGN GUIDELINES

PLE can be linked to three main divisions—resources, people, and tools—as well as to ONLE linkage designs. Individual PLEs should go beyond connecting content and human networks in addition to connect tool networks. When designing network teaching and learning, you will need an ONLE linkage design model to allow each individual to build her PLEs since course management systems do not allow the individual learner to build her own PLE. PLE's primary function is to link network tools and resources through personal portal tools, such as iGoogle. Effective personal portal linkage design also includes linking to people. Linking to people from a personal portal allows students to share their PLE experiences and to collaborate. Each gadget in iGoogle can be shared, and students can work together to achieve better learning experiences with other network learners. Additionally, by rating each gadget they use, your students will provide a good resource for other network learners to use when selecting gadgets and tools to enhance their PLEs. Using the users' ratings, called social navigation, each PLE learner can benefit each other's PLE building processes and find the gadgets and tools that best fit their needs.

To Select Network Portal Tools

Selecting a personal portal technology is the first step for applying personal portal linkage design to build a PLE, such as iGoogle, Netvibes, My Yahoo, and Microsoft Live. Regardless of which tools you select, you and your students can personalize your portal linkage to custom-build a PLE to communicate and collaborate with other learners.

Generally, the PLEs created by students are private. Some tools, such as Symbaloo and RSS, allow users to make certain parts of or their entire PLE public. When visiting a personal portal tool page, students can view different gadgets in one location that display the tools' gadget information, resources, or communications without logging on to each individual Web 2.0 tool. As instructor, consider whether the Web 2.0 tools you integrate into instructions have relevant gadgets available for your students to add to their personal portal tools. Not every Web 2.0 tool offers gadgets. However, most popular Web 2.0 tools do have gadgets for personal portal tools, such as Facebook, Twitter, Delicious, RSS, YouTube, e-mail, and calendars.

At the beginning of the class, ask students to select a personal portal tool—that is, a software program they will use for documenting and storing their learning. Be sure to appropriate ample time to assist students in selecting the tools they need. If your students have less experience with technology or in managing learning tools, consider choosing a common one for all learners to use in creating their PLEs. You can also encourage those who would like to explore different personal portal tools to build their PLEs to do so. Regardless of which tool learners select, they should not have any difficulty with communicating, sharing, and collaborating. Their selection will be more a representation of personal taste; some people use MS Word, while others use Apple's Page, Document from Google Docs, or the word processor from OpenDocument. Google plans to replace iGoogle with Google Chrome browser's apps. The readers can apply the same PLE concept suggested in this book to build their PLE on Chrome's apps. For more information on iGoogle and Chrome apps, see http:// support.google.com/websearch/bin/answer.py?hl=en&answer=2664197.

To Organize Gadgets on PLE

After they choose their personal portal tools, ask students to search, select, and organize relevant gadgets and add them to their personal portal tool. iGoogle or Symbaloo provides a good example; see http://www .symbaloo.com/mix/?q=symbaloo.

Let students know that they must add to their PLEs the gadgets required by your course, which are the Web 2.0 tools that you have integrated into your instruction, such as Google Docs, Facebook, Twitter, Google Calendar, YouTube, and e-mail. Since these tools directly relate to the instruction, it is mandatory that everyone has these gadgets on their iGoogle page. Learners should be encouraged to add additional optional gadgets to their iGoogle as well, to make their PLEs more relevant to their learning. These gadgets might include a dictionary, translator, news, bookmarks, Word of the Day, or other e-mail accounts, but they are not limited to these. For learning purposes, students can be asked to add all "required" gadgets along with an additional two or three optional gadgets to enrich their PLEs.

Within iGoogle, each Web 2.0 tool can have multiple related gadgets added—for example, Facebook gadgets. Allow students to select and add their preferred gadget, rather than requiring a specific one, unless there is a need to do so. Generally, tools such as Twitter offer multiple iGoogle gadgets. Again, allow the students to select their own gadget. This offers them a good opportunity to apply and expand their knowledge in selecting the right gadget. For example, if you're requiring a Facebook gadget, encourage students to search relevant Facebook gadgets and select one to add to their PLE. Ask them to evaluate and add different gadgets throughout the class.

After all gadgets have been added, have students reorganize them on a regular basis. All gadgets added to iGoogle can be moved and placed in any location on the iGoogle page simply by clicking and holding the banner bar of the gadget. Students can also select the layout of their iGoogle page, for example, with two or three columns.

iGoogle's "tab" feature allows learners to organize their gadgets onto multiple tabs. This can be particularly helpful when individuals would like to group their gadgets by purpose or functionality. Too many gadgets appearing in the same tab creates crowding and causes confusing PLEs. Therefore, multiple tabs are highly recommended. For example, separate tabs could be designated as Learning tab, Work tab, or Entertainment tab. On iGoogle, the same gadget can be added to multiple tabs if needed. Even if located in different tabs, the same gadgets would display the same content, resources, or communications. For example, for course learning, a PLE tab would be appropriate that would contain different course learning–related gadgets, such as Twitter gadget for course announcement, Delicious gadget for course social bookmarks and resources, Google Calendar gadget for course calendar, Google Docs gadget for course assignment files, or Google Reader for course RSS feed subscriptions.

Students can customize each tab according to their preferences. They can also change themes for different tabs and incorporate titles such as animals, Nature, Sports, and Destinations. They can even create some Fun and Trendy categories (for examples, see http://delicious.com/chihtu/SONLE +PLE+iGoogle).

iGoogle's gadgets are designed and created by the developers. If you feel a new gadget needs to be designed to support your instruction, keep in mind that anyone can design and create gadgets to share with learners or other iGoogle users. Creating a Google gadget, through Google API (see http://code.google .com/intl/en/apis/gadgets/index.html), requires more advanced technical skills.

If you are not comfortable in creating a Google gadget, consider contacting your school's or institution's technical support team or e-learning technology specialist. They may be able to assist you in creating customized Google gadgets for your instruction. Even computer science majors from the local colleges can sometimes help, and may be willing to work with you voluntarily, as part of building their school portfolio. This also offers you a good opportunity to integrate social media to get your words out, such as through Facebook or Twitter. You might even be overwhelmed by the number of responses you receive.

To Share and Collaborate on PLE

Personal portal linkage involves linking tools and resources. However, social sharing and collaboration must be integrated to enhance the effectiveness of PLE. Each individual can share gadgets with his "Friends" in his Google+ circles or others. (See iGoogle tutorials on how to share gadgets.)

Social gadgets on iGoogle are interactive types of gadgets that allow iGoogle users to view what friends are doing, share and collaborate on network tasks, or play games with each other.

Gadget rating (1–5 stars) is another way to share and to collaborate with PLEs. This refers to the users' ratings on each iGoogle gadget. The rating can function as an effective means of social navigation that supports iGoogle users in selecting the right gadgets to enhance their PLEs. Encourage students to analyze any existing gadget ratings by carefully reading the comments and then selecting the gadgets right for them. This is another great opportunity to engage students in critical thinking and practicing effective decision making. As competent community learners, students should be encouraged to provide their ratings of the gadgets they experience to support the community. The more ratings provided, the more accurate a rating will be.

To Link Tools to PLE

Although linking tools to iGoogle reside in iGoogle's gadgets, it is critical to also link iGoogle to other tools, such as Internet browsers or mobile devices via mobile apps. You can generally view iGoogle pages on any Internet browser, such as Firefox, Internet Explorer, Safari, and Chrome. Advise students to set up their iGoogle page as the home page for their browser. That way, they can immediately view and monitor instructions when they open their browsers. In addition, many mobile apps support iGoogle, so students can add iGoogle apps to their mobile devices, such as smartphones and tablets. PLE thereby becomes more mobile and supports learning anywhere and at any time.

PLE ACTIVITY DESIGNS

Simply having students set up their PLEs on their personal portal tools may not be engaging enough to support building the PLE. Here are some additional activities you might use to critically engage learners in building their PLEs.

To Create iGoogle Activities

- Ask students to create their own PLE on iGoogle or other personal portal tools at the beginning of the class.
- Have them add the gadgets that are "required" and directly related to your instruction.
- Encourage learners to add "optional" gadgets based on their needs and preferences, such as dictionary, translator, calculator, news, bookmarks, Word of the Day, and other personal e-mail account(s).

- Tell students to add relevant gadgets for the Web 2.0 tools to iGoogle when you add additional Web 2.0 tools to your instructional activity.
- Encourage them to share iGoogle gadgets with their classmates and/ or teammates.
- Inform students of iGoogle's Social gadgets that can be shared and to collaborate on learning activities. iGoogle gadgets are social if they have the social sharing icon in the top right corner. Click the icon to share social gadgets with friends.
- Ask students to demonstrate their PLEs on iGoogle with the class, either in face-to-face or online setting, so learners can learn from each other.
- Engage learners in reflecting how they may use their PLE on iGoogle to support their learning. If they are amenable, their reflections can be shared on personal or course blogs, as well as social network sites, such as Twitter or Facebook.
- At the end of the class, have students share reflections on their PLEs on iGoogle, again to enhance self-regulatory skills.
- Encourage learners to use their PLEs on iGoogle for other instructions or courses and to continue using iGoogle as PLE for future learning.
- Engage learners in integrating PLE diagrams to present, manage, and share their PLEs with other network learners (see the Chapter Learning Activity).

LINKAGE DESIGNS FOR PLE

Besides helping you connect to tools, people, and resources, you can also apply linkage design models to design more effective and comprehensive ONLE. Use each linkage model to guide and inspire yourself and your students to design effective personal portal activities. It is not necessary to integrate all linkages from the linkage design model, but do consider all linkages and determine which ones would be most effective in your instructions before making your selection.

- *RSS linkage*: Many RSS functions or RSS gadgets are available on iGoogle. You can add a specific feed to your iGoogle. Click "Add gadgets," "Add feed or gadget," "Add RSS feed URL." This feed is then added to your iGoogle page.
- *Widget linkage*: Create your own gadgets if you are tech savvy, or have support staff help, if you have access to technicians at your workplace
- *Social network linkage*: Share and collaborate with your gadgets. Integrate iGoogle's Social gadgets so students can share the gadgets with their classmates, friends, or people in their study circle.

- *Mobile linkage*: Personal portal tools are available on mobile apps, so students can access their PLE on mobile devices such as smartphones or tablets. They can also set up their own PLE on mobile devices by adding different functions of mobile apps in addition to having their PLE on iGoogle.

LEARNING ACTIVITY: CREATE PLE ON IGOOGLE

Purpose: To integrate all Web 2.0 tools in a central location with iGoogle and allow learners to monitor, manage, organize, and share/collaborate on their PLEs.

In this Learning Activity, you will apply multiple Web 2.0 tools to deliver your course instructions. Your students will build their PLEs on iGoogle by adding different iGoogle gadgets to their iGoogle page. It is recommended that you evaluate your own instructional plan to determine which Web 2.0 tools to integrate. Web 2.0 tools are frequently updated or even migrated to new tools. If the tools or gadgets discussed in this book are not available at the time you wish to integrate them, use the new ones. The key is to learn about the new tools and their integration concept. Generally, we have choices in selecting tools or gadgets. For example, in this learning activity, we introduced iGoogle; however, you can apply the same integration concept by using different PLE tools, such as Symabloo, Google Chrome apps, mobile apps, etc. These tools afford the same or similar features to personalize your learning environment.

REMINDER

If you are new to Web 2.0 integration or the linkage design model, it is highly recommended that you start by integrating just one or two tools in the beginning. When you have a better grasp of PLE, ONLE, and the linkage design model, you can integrate multiple tools. Additionally, consider your students' level of media literacy. Even if they are familiar with social media, they may or may not have experience in using Web 2.0 tools as learning tools and may not be comfortable doing this. Do not overestimate the technical skills of your students even if they seem to be familiar with the new media and technology. It is your responsibility to foster your students in developing relevant media literacy skills to support their learning, rather than assuming they have them because they use social media for personal purposes or entertainment.

Ask students to create an iGoogle account and to add any required instruction-related gadgets, such as Twitter, Google Calendar, Gmail, Google Docs, and so on. Table 8.1 depicts a list of iGoogle gadgets required for course activities. Within iGoogle, students will see all course-related and relevant gadgets. If your students are technologically savvy, consider allowing them to select different portal technologies, such as Netvibes or My Yahoo! to achieve the same functions.

- Obtain an iGoogle account: Once your Gmail account is active, use it to obtain an iGoogle account at http://www.google.com/ig. Many schools' e-mail accounts are powered by Gmail. Be sure to check with your network administrators. If learners do not have GMail, obtain it first, then the iGoogle account.
- Create a "tab" on iGoogle to hold gadgets related to instruction, and call it PLE or some other appropriate name.
- Add gadgets that are directly related to your instruction and course requirements—for example, a Twitter gadget for viewing course announcements, a Google Calendar gadget for managing course calendar, and so on. How many gadgets you add to iGoogle depends on how many Web 2.0 tools you integrate into your course and how many related gadgets are available on iGoogle. See examples at http://delicious.com/chihtu/SONLE+PLE+Image.
- Consider requiring students to add another two to three gadgets of their own choosing to their iGoogle to support their learning. These can be directly or indirectly related to your course instructions—for example, online dictionary, online translator, or news.
- Advise students to visit their iGoogle's PLE tabs regularly, perhaps every day, and to set up an iGoogle page as their home page for their browser; so when they open the browser, they can immediately view all course activities and related information on one page.
- Create multiple tabs for different personal uses. Besides the PLE tab, you can encourage students to create multiple tabs for different uses, such as for personal items, entertainment, work, or hobbies. Multiple tabs allow learners to organize their PLEs in a more efficient way, particularly when there are many gadgets to manage.
- Remind students that they must visit their iGoogle regularly to get updates on course activities, rather than visiting each Web 2.0 tool individually.
- PLE diagram exercise: Ask students to use concept mapping tools to create PLE diagrams and to share their PLE diagrams with other students via social tagging. The PLE diagram exercise allows them to visualize their PLEs and to make their PLEs more interconnected, and to improve them.
  - Concept mapping tools: There are many free concept mapping tools available online (http://delicious.com/chihtu/SONLE+PLE+Mapping). Allow students to select their own preferred concept mapping tools.
  - Create a PLE diagram: Allow students to use any style or format to create a PLE diagram that best represents their PLE.
  - Share PLE diagrams: Ask students to present their PLE diagram to other students and explain what their PLE looks like, and why their PLE diagram looks like certain features, such as linear, hierarchical, spoke, network/web designs. This show-and-tell can be conducted FTF or online.

Table 8.1   iGoogle Gadgets for Web 2.0 Technologies and Course Activities

Activities/ Assignments	Web 2.0 Tools and iGoogle Gadgets	Choices
Announcements	Gadget: Twitter	Follow the course Twitter
Assignments	Gadget: Google Docs	Students turned in assignments and received grades and feedback.
Social networking site	Gadget: Facebook	Network with classmates
Social bookmarking sharing	Gadgets: Delicious, Google Bookmarks, Diigo, Citeulike	Students' personal choices
Group projects	Gadgets: Google Site, Google Groups	Students' personal choices
Course Calendar	Gadget: Google Calendar	View course activities
E-mail	iGoogle e-mail (students' preference or Gmail)	Students' personal choices
Learning Reflections	Gadgets: Blogger, Blogosphere, etc.	Students' personal choices
Social annotation	Gadget: Diigo	Annotate course reading and share with the class.

- To capture students' PLE diagrams: Design a social tagging architecture, and require students to tag their online PLE diagrams with their choice of social tagging tools, such as Delicious or Diigo, to share with the network learning community. The tags for the social tagging architecture may include the course number, or simply be labeled as PLE or Diagram. With this approach, you can collect all students' PLE diagrams and post them to one location. See examples: http://delicious.com/chihtu/SONLE+PLE +Diagram.
- Notes: The PLE diagram should go beyond the tools used in iGoogle. If necessary, you can require your students to include mobile learning tools, notebook, friends, and other nontechnology–related tools that students use to support their learning. PLE should depict how one accesses and manages network, communication, and information from different locations, and devices for various purposes.

LAST WORDS

Social tagging resources can be seen on Delicious in chapter 1, Table 1.1.

To achieve an effective PLE, you, as instructor, need to help your students shift from online learners to network learners. Online learners are accustomed to LMS portals, which do not allow learners to manage their learning, while iGoogle requires learners to create and manage their PLEs. A perceived sense of control and high level of initiative are not enough to result in relevant self-regulatory skills, particularly regarding personal goal settings.

Ideally, you will engage students in the last-phase model of self-regulated skills and strategies, self-reflection (Zimmerman, 1998). When first creating their PLEs, students may reach the phase of forethought in self-regulated skills, given their positive motivation and perceptions of PLEs. Then they progress to the second phase of performance control related to attention, affect, and moderate monitoring of learning action. But it is not clear if they have reached the final phase of self-reflection.

Assist students with reaching the self-reflection phrase by communicating with them and ensuring their understanding of the importance of the conceptual notion of openness and interoperability in integrating iGoogle tools in their PLE's creation. Effective PLEs rely largely on learners' active management of the learning gadgets according to their goals and needs with skills and knowledge in the learning process.

CHAPTER 9

Mobilize Your Learning

Have you ever:

- Considered using your mobile device for phone calls only?
- Wondered how mobile devices could be a teaching and learning tool?
- Used only the browsers on your mobile devices?

MOBILE LINKAGE DESIGN CONCEPTS

Mobile apps linkage refers to applying mobile device apps to link to Web 2.0 tools on a smartphone or other mobile device. Mobile apps (applications) are software applications designed to run on mobile devices. They can be downloaded from application distribution platforms, such as Apple's App Store, Android Market, or BlackBerry App World. Some apps are free, while others cost money. Mobile device users can access online information and interact with other online users via mobile apps, in addition to using their Internet browsers. Many online and Web 2.0 tools also offer mobile apps, so users can access online functions in an uncomplicated and function-specific method rather than using browsers. If the instructions are delivered on Web 2.0 tools—such as Facebook, Twitter, Delicious, Facebook, RSS, Google Calendar, and QR Codes—it's also likely that these tools with their instructions can be accessed via mobile apps.

Mobile learning environments are human networks that afford learners the opportunity to participate in creative endeavors and social networking to organize or reorganize social content, and generate learner-created cognitive space (Cornelius and Marston, 2009) as well as manage social acts anytime and anywhere through mobile technologies. Social acts that elicit identities, develop awareness (Kekwaletswe, 2007), cement relationships, ensure connections, and promote interactions between and among learners are necessary components of interactive learning.

Social interaction with mobile technology differs substantially from computer-mediated communication (CMC) or Web 2.0 networking technologies. Researchers (Koole, McQuilkin, and Ally, 2010) are aware that through human interaction on mobile technology, both the user and the technology are shaping each other. Mobile technology connects learners virtually anytime and anywhere, while mobile learners use it in nontraditional ways to interact with each other (Kukulska-Hulme and Traxler, 2007). Research has shown that mobile technology has impacted human social relationships (Jones and Issroff, 2007) and interaction both positively and negatively (Rau, Gao, and Wu, 2008). Mobile learning involves more than just integrating mobile devices and mobile technologies into your instruction. Mobile learning from an instructional perspective should be integrated from four vantage points: mobile technology, mobile learners, mobile teachers, and mobile instructions.

More than just replicating desktop and laptop computing, mobile linkage design focuses on social-context awareness via integrating location-based technology, which is unique to mobile technology. It is easy to integrate most Web 2.0 tools and linkage designs into mobile learning. With the features of location-based technology or Global Positioning System (GPS), mobile learners are able to obtain content and enrich their learning environment. For example, with mobile devices, learners can access online information specifically related to their current location; they can access nearby social network friends to collaborate on learning tasks; and they can record data, such as photos, audio, video, environmental information, with embedded geo-location data. Mobile learning with mobile apps linkage design fulfills learning in a more ubiquitous manner, with richer social awareness that is more personalized and within more meaningful contexts.

Rather than seeing students' mobile devices as a distracting technology, consider transforming them into learning devices and tools. Your institution may not have resources to provide each student with a computer, but even if it did, computers are not personalized enough, are not mobile, and are not context-specific enough, when compared to mobile technology, to enhance learning in innovative ways.

MOBILE APPS DESIGN GUIDELINES

In this chapter, we focus on the general features and design of mobile apps, rather than on each mobile app's specific functions. These general features allow mobile users to access tools or websites without using a browser. Generally, users can use mobile apps to perform whatever features or designs the tools or websites offer. More specific functions for mobile apps may vary, such as log-in requirement and free or paid app functions.

To Select Mobile Apps

Many mobile apps are available for different mobile operating systems (OS). Selecting the right apps to support your teaching is critical. Many apps are free, while others range from less a dollar to relatively expensive. Here are a few guidelines for selecting apps to assist you in your teaching and learning.

- For any given function, you may find multiple apps. For example, there are many apps available for Twitter, Facebook, RSS, and To Do List. Try out some different apps to see which best meets your needs—especially if they are free. You can delete any unwanted items and add preferred apps.
- Consult "Review" information to assist you in selecting a right app. All app stores have this information. Generally, they are arranged in five-star review scales. Be sure to read other users' review notes. This is particularly important when the apps are not free, although many apps are inexpensive.
- Use "Top Charts" to help you screen for selection of the best apps. Generally, app stores list top paid apps or top free apps.
- Additional features: generally, apps have the basic functions you need. Do not overlook the additional features in the apps, such as embedded location-based technology and social networking features for advanced collaboration.
- Augmented reality (AR) "is a live, direct or indirect, view of a physical, real-world environment whose elements are augmented by computer-generated sensory input such as sound, video, graphics or GPS data" (Augmented Reality, 2013, para 1). This is a feature you don't generally find in other computing devices. Even when you do, the device may not be portable enough to be used in the field. Many apps have an embedded AR feature, while some specifically focus on AR features.
- Network with people informed about mobile apps to keep up with the best new apps.
- Allow students to select their own mobile apps, as long as they can be linked to the planned one and can accomplish the same required tasks. Generally, this can be determined through sharing their app activities via social network sites. By allowing students to select their favorite apps, you are providing them with another effective learning activity.

To Organize Mobile Apps

Since apps can be easily downloaded and many of them are free, they tend to accumulate. Therefore, it's essential that you strategically organize your apps. Most mobile OSs have multiple pages and folders features. You can organize your apps in the following ways:

- Page organization: Create different pages for apps with similar uses or functions.
- Folder organization: If you prefer less page navigation, apply the folder organization feature and organize apps with similar functions or uses into a folder, named with a title that is meaningful to you.

SHARE AND COLLABORATE WITH MOBILE APPS

There are two types of sharing and collaborating with mobile apps: within apps and by sharing them.

- Share and collaborate within apps: Many apps have embedded social networking features that allow you to share and collaborate on your app activities within your friends' network. For example, within photo apps, you can share the photos on your mobile devices with your network friends by e-mailing them; or you can share the photos with other Web 2.0 tools, such as Facebook, Twitter, and Flickr. The sharing feature can also advance collaborative learning by encouraging student groups to share the data or information they gather on their mobile devices. Since many apps have embedded location-based technology, the collaborative data contains other layers of information. Some apps integrate location-based technology to deliver AR functions. For example, Public Broadcasting Service's (PBS) AR mobile app, FETCH! Lunch Rush, overlays computer-generated graphics on top of the physical, real-world environment. It is a 3-D game, which helps children visualize the math problems they are trying to solve. The purpose of this AR mobile app is to use media to nurture children's natural curiosity and inspire them to explore the world around them. See http://pbskids.org/mobile/fetch-lunch-rush.html.
- Sharing apps: There are many apps in app stores, and sharing our favorite apps with our network friends is a great way to learn about new apps. On your iOS (internetwork operation system) device, you can share an app from the app store directly with your network by finding and clicking on the application you want. Then select "Tell a Friend," which allows you to e-mail your friend with a link to the application. On an Android device, open the Android Market and select the

app you would like to share, click "Share this Application," and either
e-mail, text, or Facebook message. If you have multiple apps you would
like to share, consider using "Applist.me," which allows you to share a
list of iOS apps with your network friends. It is a free application that
you can download to both Mac and Windows computers.

To Link Tools Mobile Linkage

Effective linkage designs use mobile apps that link to different mobile
devices and tools. Rarely do mobile apps function alone. If you are using a
mobile app only on your mobile device, consider looking for the ability to
link it to different devices or tools to make it more effective.

- Some apps are available on multiple devices or mobile OS. If you use
  certain apps on specific mobile devices, look for the same apps on your
  other mobile devices, or on a mobile OS. Most apps are available for
  different mobile devices and different mobile OSs. On Mac computers,
  there is an App Store with apps that regular computers can download.
- You can link apps to another person's tools. When using certain
  apps, examine whether the apps have a sharing feature. If yes, you
  can share the app data with your network friends via e-mail, Facebook, Twitter, or other popular social network sites.
- Apps data and information can also be shared and posted to other
  Web 2.0 tools. For example, you can post the app data to Facebook,
  Twitter, Flickr, or Delicious.
- You can link to location-based technology. Examine whether the
  apps have embedded location-based technology that has the potential to apply augmented reality to enhance learning in more meaningful real-time, context-specific, location-specific ways. When
  opening an app, you may find a question like "Would like to use
  your current location." If so, you know your app has embedded
  location-based technology. For AR apps, search the term "augmented reality" in any app store.

MOBILE LINKAGE ACTIVITY DESIGNS

To Create Mobile Apps Activities

- Create activities that infuse virtual and physical worlds to enhance
  learning and take advantage of the mobility aspect of the technology.
- Create activities that engage students in social sharing and collaboration via their mobile devices.
- Create activities that allow students to share their favorite apps.

MOBILE LINKAGE DESIGNS

Mobile apps are fairly compatible with other Web 2.0 tools and mobile devices and can create opportunities for teachers to apply linkage designs to link people, resources, and tools. Avoid using one app for a single purpose.

Below are a few suggestions for applying linkages to enhance your mobile app instructions.

- *Personal portal linkage*: The standard personal learning environment may have been created on iGoogle or with other tools, but with so many mobile apps for Web 2.0 tools, you can easily support your teaching by adding and organizing different apps. With relevant apps, you and your students can perform almost identical tasks on your mobile devices as on your computers.
- *RSS linkage*: If a Web 2.0 tool doesn't have mobile app, check whether it has RSS. If it does, you can download an RSS app and subscribe to the RSS feed; that way, you can access the tool's RSS feed on mobile devices.
- *Third-party linkage*: iTunes must be downloaded to your computer, thereby allowing you to link your mobile apps to your computer, even if mobile apps do not require a connection to a computer to perform app functions. With iTunes, you can organize and back up your downloaded apps.
- *Widget linkage*: Mobile apps function like widgets. We call these browser-based software programs widgets, while we call mobile OS software mobile apps. In other words, we use widget linkage for browser-based functions, while we use mobile apps linkage for mobile devices.
- *Social tagging linkage*: Many social bookmarking tools have mobile apps (e.g., Delicious, Diigo).
- *Social network linkage*: Most apps have embedded social networking features, so users can share their apps data, information, or activities with others via social network sites or e-mail, and so on.
- *InfoViz linkage*: InfoViz linkage allows you to monitor your mobile device usage. There are many apps available to monitor mobile device activity and usage and display the results in a visual format. This is particularly useful if users' mobile device activities are being collected for research purposes. Some apps have built-in InfoViz feature that analyzes your app activities, such as mapping your exercise route on an overlapping map or showing you various exercise data. When selecting apps, watch for those with built-in InfoViz features. When searching an app store, use "data usage monitor" as search keywords.

LEARNING ACTIVITY:
EXPLORING AND COLLABORATING WITH MOBILE APPS

Purpose: To engage students in interactive mobile learning

Instructions: Explore two teaching scenarios. The first one involves integrating mobile apps in a file to allow students to collaborate. The second engages students in interactive analysis, selection, and effective sharing of mobile apps with others.

Case I:
Mobile Social Networking for Museum Scavenger Hunt

Social networking linkage extended with mobile learning can also enhance field learning. In this scenario, students visit museums or other venues outside of the classroom to collect and share learning resources with their group and the class through social networking on mobile apps. This scavenger hunt could occur during or outside of schooltime. Students can work with their social networking group to complete the tasks.

- Tools: mobile devices such as smartphones, tablets, iPod Touch, or any portable device with Wi-Fi capability.
- Applications, mobile apps: Foursquare, SCVNGR, Facebook, Gowalla and others can be used. In this case, we will use Foursquare.

Before you go on the field trip, set up and configure all the devices that will be used and check what is available at the site—for example, Wi-Fi, student access, use policies, and so on.

- Download Foursquare Apps to your mobile device, and have students do the same. See https://foursquare.com/. It is free.
- Create your own account. You and the students will then create an account on Foursquare, following instructions on the site.
- Visit the site of your field trip. During this advance visit, you need to do a few things that require checking with the staff at the facility:
  - Take your mobile device with you.
  - Check with the site manager about using Foursquare. The site manager will likely have a list of check-in locations on Foursquare for their site.
  - Walk through the museum and visit every single section that you would like your students to visit, and collect the information on the museum displays. At each check-in location, post the tasks or instructions to the Foursquare that you would like your students to perform.

If a check-in location is not available, create your own check-in points for your students.

- If your students are using mobile devices that your institution has provided, be sure to have your school technicians reset the mobile device to the school's configurations.
- If you do not have enough mobile devices for every student, allow one device for each group, and supplement them with loaned devices or students' personal devices.
- Provide a workshop in advance to assist students in understanding the goals of the scavenger hunt activity, and help them learn to navigate and manage their mobile devices.
- Engage students in device setup and exercise activities.
  - Explain the purposes of this activity.
  - Download Foursquare account to the mobile devices.
  - Create accounts for Foursquare.
    - If all students have mobile devices, each of them should create his own account. If not, each group should share one account.
    - If you have privacy concerns for your students, consider advising them to use pseudonyms for their account. In that case, be sure to obtain the account information from each student or group.
    - Social networking with Foursquare accounts: All students and groups should network with you by becoming friends. If each student has her own device, students in the same group should become friends as well, so they can collaborate in a more specific context. With you and your students networked, you can easily observe their Foursquare activities. In Foursquare, friends can view friends' activities, providing a better opportunity to collaborate.
    - Conduct an exercise to familiarize students with how to use Foursquare for the activities. The exercise allows students to check in at different locations in the school for a simple scavenger hunt.
  - Explain the instructions and tasks that you would like your students to perform at the museum.

Reminder: The key in this design is social networking between you, students, and groups, so your class or class groups can share and collaborate on their learning in a more specific rather than public context.

TIPS

While visiting a museum or in the field, you may want to know exactly where your students are. You can integrate the Augmented Reality app to locate your students.

- Select an AR app, such as Wikitude.
- Download the app to all student mobile devices

- Have all students and groups become friends on Facebook.
- Ask students or groups to update their Facebook feed or Twitter feed. For example, you can ask them to give you a short progress report every hour.
- Aim your mobile device in different directions to view which students or groups are updating their Facebook or Twitter feed.

After locating certain students or groups, check in with them directly for their progress reports.

Case II:
Analyze and Share Mobile Apps

Since there are so many apps available for mobile devices, it is impossible for any individual teacher to search them all and select apps for their courses. Why not engage students in the activities of apps searching, analyzing, and sharing, particularly in applying Bloom's Revised Taxonomy (Schrock, 2012), Remembering, Understanding, Applying, Evaluating, and Creating, to analyze mobile apps. In this exercise, you will use Google Form to create an online form that allows your students to analyze and share mobile apps with others.

- Create a Google Form to collect students' input on app analysis. See the example at https://spreadsheets.google.com/spreadsheet/viewform?hl=e-n_US&formkey=dE9kYVpwMGpLa1pfVmlBbVlvVXJQVl E6MQ#gid=0.
- If needed, add more fields to collect aspects of students' app analysis that are useful to your teaching, such as rating of the apps, usefulness, ease of use, and price.
- If you like, on Google Form, you can check "Show summary of responses." This enables students to view the results input by their classmates.
- If there are certain levels of taxonomy that lack input, encourage students to submit app analysis on those.
- If needed, allow students to discuss their analysis of apps during class.

TIPS

Here are a few more tips for you to plan this app analysis activity.

- Collaborate with other teachers who may be doing something similar; that way, you can collect and collaborate more and more meaningful app analysis data.
- Continue collecting the app analysis from semester to semester so current students can learn from previous students' contributions.

Make a game of this activity. For example, for each app analysis students submit, they can earn points, badges, or other trophies.

LAST WORDS

Social tagging resources can be seen on Delicious in chapter 1, Table 1.1.

Mobile devices for schools are often seen as distractions from classroom learning. Why not creatively integrate them to support teaching and learning? Many students have their own mobile devices already, and mobile devices cost even less for schools. It is likely that all students have access to these devices. Remember, it is not necessary that all students have devices; they can be used with groups as well.

Mobile learning does not just replicate traditional learning; and it should be used in ways that exploit its capabilities. For example, it would not be productive to have students complete a written paper on their mobile devices. Mobile learning should be integrated from the unique features provided by mobile technology and mobile apps, such as social sharing and collaborating, audio and video recording, and location-based technology. These features are not generally found on computers. Additionally, since mobile devices are universally transportable, students can access these devices and apps anytime and anywhere.

KEY LINKING THINKING

- Is there a mobile app for a certain Web 2.0 tool?
- Is there an app for something I want to teach or learn?
- Can I share/collaborate/link the apps with other tools or devices?
- Does the app have location-based technology to enrich social learning?

PART V

COGNITIVE DIMENSION

Part V focuses on learning processes and development through creating, editing, and remixing learning content, socially and collaboratively.

CHAPTER 10

Make Your World Flat

Have you ever:

- Considered how blog, Twitter, or Facebook discussions differ from online threaded discussion boards?
- Wondered if blog, Twitter, or Facebook discussions might allow you to see who is talking to whom?

FLAT-STRUCTURED DISCUSSION DESIGN CONCEPTS

Have you been integrating an online or threaded discussion board to enhance your teaching? Have you used Twitter or other Web 2.0 tools' discussion feature as discussion boards? If so, you may have noticed that Web 2.0 discussion boards work very differently from threaded discussion boards.

Online discussion boards offer some of the most effective instructional strategies to engage learners in knowledge construction and to teach critical thinking skills (Cheong and Cheung, 2008; de Leng et. al., 2009). Educators today integrate asynchronous online discussion boards into their instruction to enhance learning in completely online, hybrid, or web-enhanced instructions because it works. Research confirms this, showing that online discussions support learners and instructors to challenge, reform, and synthesize

Portions of this chapter were previously published by Chih-Hsiung Tu, Michael Blocher, and Lawrence Gallagher, "The Examination of Flat-Structured Discussions as Organizational Scaffold Learning," *Journal of Educational Technology Development and Exchange*, 3(1) 2010: 43–56.

their current views of knowledge through in-depth interaction with other learners (Garrison, Anderson, and Archer, 2001). Researchers agree that asynchronous online discussions frame a constructivist learning approach and enhance interaction, analysis, and collaboration of discussion participants (Bonk and Dennen, 2007), as well as build critical thinking skills (Richardson and Ice, 2010). More specifically, research has concluded that asynchronous threaded discussions effectively facilitate learners' metacognitive awareness and development of self-regulatory processes and strategies (Vonderwell, Liang, and Alderman, 2007).

Online asynchronous discussion boards are frequently conducted in a text-based format as threaded, tree, nested, or parent-child interface. Often asynchronous online discussion boards are integrated with an LMS, such as Blackboard or Moodle. These online discussion activities are generally initiated by instructors as course requirements, where learners must reply to discussion questions and/or others' postings individually or in groups.

Since the advent of Web 2.0 tools, many educators have started to integrate Web 2.0 discussion boards to support their online discussions or to replace threaded discussion boards. In general, Web 2.0 discussion boards apply a "flat-structured" format to display the discussion postings chronologically, along with additional social network features, such as tagging, RSS, widgets, tag clouds, and social network linkages. A flat-structured discussion board applies a simple interface; all postings are displayed in a single level, rather than in a threaded or nested reply structure. Flat-structured discussion formats are frequently found in blogs, wikis, and social network sites (Twitter, Facebook, Ning). (See the example at https://www.facebook.com/Forum ForPages.)

Because the technology is new to them, educators often integrate Web 2.0's flat-structured discussions without fully understanding the different interface features. Web 2.0 offers some advantages to flat-structured discussions that can potentially enhance online discussion with more engaging and personal designs, such as switching different views on discussion board or RSS subscriptions

These two different discussion formats, threaded and flat, use different interfaces to display online discussion postings. Tu, Blocher, and Gallagher (2010) identified that both threaded and flat-structured discussion formats impacted learners' discussion experiences in thinking, density of discussion context, context-oriented discussion environments, social network features, social tagging, network mechanisms, collaborative effectiveness, and community sense. Both formats empower discussion among participants, but in different ways; and with strategic designs, they engage learners in more meaningful, deeper, and higher-order thinking. To argue that one is better or more effective than the other, or to dispute that educators should seek the potential of applying one tool to replace the other, misses the point.

LEARNING IMPACTS

Human thinking, knowledge presentations, and constructions are not as simple as hierarchical, linear, or threaded forms. Human thinking is better symbolized in a more networked, woven format (Educause, 2008). In other words, humans reflect and synthesize various types of ideas/viewpoints to construct a new set of understandings. Hillman, Willis, and Gunawardena (1994) emphasized the importance of learner-interface interaction. Branching and replying cause threaded discussions to veer off track; and following a thread that has branched can be discombobulating and unnatural, which commonly forces participants to initiate a new thread if and when they want to return to the initial topic. Flat-structured discussions require participants to read all postings to promote metacognition and self-regulated skills to achieve higher learning.

WEAVING AND SYNTHESIZING POSTINGS

Educators would likely agree that synthesizing various posted ideas and viewpoints into one coherent position in online discussions would be more valuable than replying to a single idea or viewpoint at a time. To achieve a synthesizing function in a threaded discussion, online learners view the content of each posting to determine which ones require a response. Before online learners can synthesize the contents of a threaded interface, they are forced to search and peck, which can easily defuse their thinking. Typically, participants read several postings and select one that seems appropriate for response, inducing parent-child postings. Participants tend not to read every posting before they reply (Feldstein, 2005). In this way, the approach of reading one and replying to one becomes common in threaded discussions.

AUTHENTIC LEARNER-CENTERED LEARNING

Learners follow the hierarchical and threaded structures in threaded discussions to construct their knowledge through limited learner-centered learning. Flat-structured discussions require learners to organize, manage, and regulate their own discussion learning structures by using other social and network mechanisms. This is a more authentic, learner-centered experience where learners are empowered to shape learning technology. To thoroughly understand the activities of flat-structured discussions, learners must organize and manage the discussion activities based on their preferences; otherwise, the discussion postings could become disorganized or overwhelming. For example, learners must apply different viewing formats to view the flat-structured discussion postings, or tag the discussion postings to help them to organize the posting content.

Current literature indicates several weaknesses in the threaded discussion format. Research has also shown that flat-structured discussion formats have the potential to resolve the weaknesses of threaded discussions. Educators should not overlook integrating a flat-structured format to improve online discussion instructions. It is essential that you as instructor have a comprehensive understanding of your students' learning experiences in both discussion formats.

FLAT-STRUCTURED DISCUSSION DESIGN GUIDELINES

To Select a Features-Rich Discussion Board

Currently, many discussion boards have both threaded and flat features for displaying discussion postings. A discussion board with both display features is more effective, since participants can determine which format they prefer for viewing discussion postings; or they can use both. This helps them follow the discussion development and make better decisions about responding to postings. In addition to the chronological display interface, flat-structured discussions are normally equipped with optional and additional social network features, such as social tagging, tag clouds, RSS, widgets, receiving and posting from e-mails, social network linkages, and mobile learning linkages that allow discussion participants to access and understand discussion content from different perspectives not available in a threaded format. Of course, you must still integrate these tools as a course requirement to ensure that participants utilize them to support online discussions.

To Organize Flat-Structured Discussions

Flat-structured discussion boards generally include other networking technologies to help support learning, such as RSS and social tagging feature. This allows you to achieve a better organizational scaffold to engage learners. Flat-structured discussion boards are, in their raw format, arranged chronologically. As mentioned, chronological formats can present difficulties in comprehending discussion contents. To counteract those difficulties, require your students to integrate RSS (Lee, Miller, and Newnham, 2008) and social tagging (Godwin-Jones, 2006) and to use them to integrate the discussion postings into their own organized structures. This way, online learners will define their own organizational learning scaffold rather than following the predetermined hierarchical structures.

To Share and Collaborate within Flat-Structured Discussions

Unlike a threaded discussion board, a flat-structured discussion board can usually function within open or closed environments. In a more open discussion board, a flat-structured discussion generally has an RSS feature that provides opportunities for collaborating with other students or sharing tools. Online learners and instructors can also easily share any postings to other social media, such as Twitter and Facebook.

Generally, flat-structured discussion boards do not expire unless the administrator decides to close it; therefore, the contributions are not flushed out, and the postings become digital cognition prints of the participants. A digital cognition footprint is the sum of activities and behavior on shared content, resources, comments, postings, and reflections recorded as an entity interacts in a digital environment, such as Web 2.0 tools. In other words, the participants' contributions to the discussion stay with the participants on the discussion boards.

To Link Tools to a Flat-Structured Discussion Board

Flat-structured discussion boards provide a more open network environment; they are fairly compatible with other social networking tools and digital devices. Before you design your flat-structured discussion board, evaluate its capability with other tools, such as e-mail, mobile apps, and mobile devices. Many flat-structured discussion boards allow users to subscribe to the discussion by posting via e-mail. When any new postings occur, the subscribers receive an e-mail with the posted text. Some discussion boards have a feature that allows users to reply to the e-mail notification and to post their response without visiting the actual discussion boards. This feature gives users more control over their own PLE.

Additionally, most threaded discussion boards are available on mobile devices' browsers, but not on mobile apps. Flat-structured discussion boards, such as blogs, Twitter, Facebook, Nabble, and Diigo, have designated mobile apps available for mobile devices, such as smartphones and tablets. With mobile apps, discussion connectedness and participation become easier, more ubiquitous, and learning context is more specific. Mobile apps are designed for more specific functions as opposed to general purposes like browsers. Mobile apps offer the advantage of interactivity, personalization, native functionality or processing required, and no Internet connection is necessary in some apps. Additionally, with mobile apps, discussion participants can share postings, pictures, video, and other data they cannot access with computers. Clearly, this is an advantage that typical threaded discussion boards cannot offer.

FLAT-STRUCTURED DISCUSSION ACTIVITY DESIGNS

Many instructors integrate flat-structured discussion boards into their courses with the concept of a threaded discussion format. This is a trap to avoid. If you integrate flat-structure with a threaded discussion concept, the flat-structured discussion becomes just another discussion board and will likely result in less interactive learning than with the threaded format. When integrating the flat-structured format into your course, focus on the unique features and designs this format offers, and take advantage of them.

Flat-structured discussions:

- Offer learners the opportunity to participate while maintaining their PLE.
- Support mobile learning.
- Allow learners to maintain their digital cognition prints.
- Engage learners in social networking rather than just content discussions.
- Allow learners to manage and administrate their discussion postings.

LINKAGE DESIGNS FOR FLAT-STRUCTURED DISCUSSION

Even though a flat-structured discussion board is not directly related to any specific linkage, it is important to apply it to your linkage design model to make the flat-structured discussion board more personalized and effective.

Below are a few ways for you to apply flat-structured discussion board to linkages and thereby enhance your flat-structured discussion instructions.

- *Personal portal linkage*: Since flat-structured discussion boards often are compatible with e-mail, RSS, mobile apps, and mobile devices, you and your students can set up your personal portals so you can monitor, review, and participate in discussion boards from those portals, without visiting the actual discussion board sites. As long as you visit your personal portals regularly, you can be connected to the discussion board and participate in the discussion from them.
- *RSS linkage*: Almost all flat-structured discussion boards have RSS features that make the discussion board more accessible on different devices and through different portals and display formats. You and your students can view and participate in discussions via mobile RSS apps on your mobile devices. RSS feeds can be linked to different InfoViz tools, such as Wordle or Dipity; and discussion boards can be displayed on personal portals with RSS feeds.
- *Widget linkage*: Web 2.0 widget technologies allow participants to link to or embed flat-structured discussions into different web pages, wiki pages, and personal portals, such as iGoogle (http://igoogle .com), Symbaloo (http://www.symbaloo.com/), as well as to mobile apps and devices. These social networking technologies allow

participants to sign on, manage, and organize flat-structured discussions at their preferred locations and with the technologies at hand (e.g., mobile devices).

- *Social tagging linkage*: Flat-structured discussions generally allow participants to tag their postings in a field separate from the postings. These tags function as keywords for organization and search purposes. Participants can provide tags based on their posting content or social context to enrich the postings. Some tools may feature a tag cloud or a word cloud, which allows participants to view multiple tags based on the frequency of tags, depicting the more frequently used tags with larger fonts.

- *Social linkage*: Unlike threaded discussions, flat-structured discussions can visually display participants' names and profiles, including such features as pictures, avatars, and links to personal profiles along with their postings. Participants can upload their own pictures or avatars, configure their personal profiles, or network to become friends, fans, or followers. Every time participants post, their pictures or avatars are attached to their postings, along with links to their profiles. This feature provides a visual interface to support discussions with more social and personal touches and effects. To view the authors' profile, participants usually need just click the pictures or avatars. Some flat-structured discussion boards are equipped with widgets that automatically feature community highlights—for example, hot topics, top discussion contributors, and visual highlights of members. Network servers power these social network mechanisms, and they display discussion activities based on real-time data from different perspectives.

- *Mobile linkage*: Mobile linkage involves the applications of mobile apps, rather than browser access on mobile devices. Many flat-structured discussion boards have designated apps that make the discussion easier and more convenient to monitor and participate in. Be sure to examine the discussion board you intend to integrate into your course, and find out whether it has mobile apps available. For example, Twitter, Facebook, blogs, Diigo, and Nabble through RSS subscriptions have mobile apps available on different mobile operation systems, such as Android or iOS.

- *InfoViz linkage*: The social tagging and RSS features of flat-structured discussion boards can be integrated with InfoViz tools to make the discussion board more visual and more engaging than the traditional text-based formats. Many discussion boards have RSS feed features that can be linked to Wordle, and timeline tools, such as Dipity, to display discussion postings in word clouds and visual timeline formats to enhance the discussions.

**LEARNING ACTIVITY:
OPEN NETWORK DISCUSSION BOARD: ENGAGING WITHOUT VISITING**

Purpose: To integrate flat-structured discussion boards into the design of PLE.

Instructions: In this Learning Activity, you will integrate Nabble, a flat-structured discussion board, for network discussion activities that are enhanced by different linkage designs—for example, personal portal linkage, RSS linkage, widget linkage, social tagging, mobile app linkage, and InfoViz linkage. Simply having effective network discussion tools does not necessarily result in completely effective learning environments. Effective instructional strategies should also be developed and integrated into network discussion activities.

In this Learning Activity, you apply multiple Web 2.0 tools to the Nabble discussion board to engage learners in ONLEs. See Table 10.1.

Table 10.1   Using Multiple Web 2.0 Tools with Nabble Discussion Board

Course instructions	Delivery tools
Online discussions	Nabble
E-mail	Any e-mail
Personal portal	iGoogle, Symbaloo, Mobile apps, Google Chrome apps
Mobile device	Any mobile devices, such as smartphones or tablets (Android phones, iPhones, etc.)
Course activity timeline	Dipity
Word clouds for discussion board	Wordle

Setting Up Your Nabble Discussion Board

Setting up a Nabble discussion board is fairly straightforward and easy, so not much explanation is offered here. See http://n4.nabble.com/free-forum.html. Instead, we focus on how you can design a Nabble discussion board and integrate it with your ONLE and PLE instructional strategies.

Recommended Linkage Design Integrations

Most instructors who teach online use online discussion boards for their online discussions. Only rarely are discussion boards integrated with other tools and instructional strategies. This Learning Activity offers an alternative approach to the typical online discussion activities. Instructors and students take more control of their discussion activities. Rather than just visit the discussion board, read postings, and reply to postings, instructors and students manage and organize the discussion postings, and can review and participate in discussions anywhere and anytime via their mobile devices. They can also apply a different visual format to help them understand the discussion postings.

Reviewing and Participating in a Discussion Board via E-mail

Nabble discussion boards have e-mail subscription features that allow discussion board participants to subscribe to the discussion postings via e-mail. When someone posts, the participants receive an e-mail that contains the posted message. Participants can then simply respond to the e-mail in reply to the discussion board posting without visiting the actual discussion board. As long as they visit their e-mail account regularly, they can monitor and participate in the discussions. In this case, e-mail becomes part of the PLE.

Here is the process to subscribe to a discussion topic:

- Create a discussion topic.
- Open the discussion topic.
- Select "Options" from the top right corner.
- Select "Subscribe via email."
- Click "Save Subscription."

Reviewing and Participating via RSS Feed Subscription

The Nabble discussion board is also equipped with RSS feeds for the entire forum or each subforum.

Here is how to subscribe:

- Find the forum RSS feed on the Nabble discussion board created on the lower-left corner labeled as "Feeds."
- Visit the forum or the subforum of your choice.
- Click "Feeds" button, located on the lower-left corner of the forum.
- Select either "Topics only" or "Topics and replies."
- Copy the RSS feed URL.
- Paste the RSS feed URL to your preferred RSS reader, such as Outlook RSS feed subscription, or Internet browser RSS feeds.

Using a Personal Portal to Manage the Discussions

A personal portal, such as iGoogle, can be a good tool to centralize all learning tasks and activities, especially if you are already using iGoogle for other learning tasks and activities. iGoogle offers different e-mail gadgets and RSS gadgets. You and your students can use either e-mail or RSS gadgets to subscribe to Nabble discussion board postings.

Applying the Timeline Format to Understand Discussion Activities

Nabble discussion boards can be displayed in Classic, List, and Threaded formats, which can all be accessed on the upper-left hand corner of the discussion topic view. Classic and List are in flat-structured formats. Classic provides full posting view, and List provides a summary view with only the author's name and subject field. By integrating Nabble's RSS feature and using tools such as Dipity, you can display discussion boards in an interactive and dynamic, visually engaging digital timeline format. This format enhances the discussion board with easier participation, sharing, and collaboration, which all helps create a more engaging discussion.

The steps are:

- Obtain (copying and pasting) the Nabble discussion board or topic RSS feeds.
- Visit Dipity (creating an account if you haven't already).
- Create a topic on Dipity. (This could relate to the course, the training, or any learning unit that you are designing.)
- Visit the Dipity topic just created.
- Select "Show Sources" below the timeline.
- Select "Edit Source List."
- Select "Other" from the left navigation menu
- Select "Any RSS Feed."
- Post the obtained RSS feed URL to the URL field.
- Select "Import from RSS URL."
- Select "Save and View Timeline"
- View the postings that appear in the timeline, if any.
- Click any posting on the timeline to view the entire message posting without visiting the Nabble discussion board.

(For more information on Dipity, see chapter 12.)

Employing Word Clouds to Examine the Discussion Postings

Nabble discussion postings can also be displayed in a word cloud format, such as Wordle, to help the discussion participants better understand what has been discussed. Wordle generates "word clouds that give greater prominence to words that appear more frequently in the source text" (Feinberg, 2013, para 1). Viewing discussion postings in a word cloud format provides a different way to understand the discussion content. See the example at http://www.wordle.net/show/wrdl/5210010/Word_Cloud_for_Online _Discussions.

Steps are:

- Obtain (copying and pasting) the Nabble discussion board or topic RSS feeds.
- Visit Wordle.net.
- Select "Create your own."
- Copy and paste the RSS feed URL to the field of "Enter the URL of any blog, blog feed, or any other web page that has an Atom or RSS feed."
- Click "Submit."

There are many ONLE/PLE instructional strategies that you can integrate to enhance your online discussion boards. Below are a few additional suggestions. They are arranged according to different learning dimensions: cognitive, social, network, and integration.

In the area of *cognitive dimension*, the following instructional strategies are recommended:

- Provide warm-up exercises for the discussion board before any graded discussions take place.
- Explain the different values for both discussion formats.
- Explain that both discussion formats require different mental models to construct knowledge.
- Encourage or require social tags.
- Integrate learner moderation to enhance a higher level of learning responsibility.
- Require learners to create, manage, and organize network discussions of their own through their PLE on a personal web portal, such as iGoogle, e-mail, any RSS readers, or NetVibes.

In the area of *social dimension*, the following instructional strategies are recommended:

- Encourage or require students to create their own profiles and share their pictures or avatars to enrich the social context.
- Encourage learners to join social networks by requesting entry as friends, fans, or followers. (Note: Nabble does not have this feature. If you use other sites, consider integrating social networking feature.)
- Apply a third-party social network tool such as Google +, Facebook, or Twitter to support social relationships among learners and instructors.
- Apply social network widgets, such as Top Contributors or Member Highlights, to tighten social bonding. (Note: Nabble does not have this feature; however, it does offer similar functions to sort the discussion board participants by the numbers of their posting. See Main Nabble discussion board "People," located upper left).

In the area of *networking dimension*, the following instructional strategies are recommended:

- Provide social tagging strategies. Encourage or require students to update the subject field when replying to any postings; that way, the subject fields become more meaningful. Otherwise, the subject fields appear as "Re:Re:Re" after a few replies.
- Require or encourage course members to subscribe to RSS feed(s) for the discussions.
- Require or encourage students to subscribe to the discussion board via e-mail, so they receive any new postings in their e-mail. Students can reply

to any posting by replying to the discussion board post e-mail without visiting the discussion board.

- Require or encourage learners to integrate RSS readers (e.g., RSS feeds into Synbaloo) to organize discussion postings.
- Encourage students to use mobile devices to access the discussion board. Nabble discussion boards have RSS and e-mail subscription features, so students can access the discussion board via mobile RSS and e-mail apps on their mobile devices, rather than using mobile browsers.
- Apply tag and/or word clouds to support discussions with visual information and depictions.
- Provide tutorials for subscribing to RSS, social tagging, and other social and networking mechanisms.
- Apply other Web 2.0 tools to organize discussion board postings. For example, consider linking the postings to personal blogs with widget or RSS feeds, social bookmarking (Delicious), social networking site (Facebook), social annotation (Diigo), or PLE (Symbaloo).
- Select tools with multiple formats (threaded, nested, flat, audio, video, and mobile) and multiple social network features to create ONLE to allow students to manage and organize their PLE.

In the area of *integration dimension*, the following instructional strategies are recommended:

- Design and engage learners in collaborative network discussion activities.
- Integrate student group moderations into discussions to promote a collaborative learning community. Divide students into groups and assign each group with discussion moderator responsibilities to facilitate discussion activities.
- Encourage peer support by creating peer support discussion boards, where students can post questions and allow others to respond.
- Ask students to save copies of their postings or the discussion thread for their own records and to serve as their digital cognition print.

LAST WORDS

Social tagging resources can be seen on Delicious in chapter 1, Table 1.1.

Both threaded and flat-structured discussion formats can critically enhance and constrain online discussions of students. Both formats empower participants in different ways and help engage them in a more meaningful, deeper, and higher order of thinking.

The issue is not whether to use one more or one less tool for teaching, because learning can occur with either. Instead, ask yourself these questions: What are the most effective ways I can engage learners in active interaction in online discussions? How can I engage learners in active learning by managing, organizing, and making more effective knowledge constructions in the online discussion learning processes? What tools should be used, and how should these tools be integrated to enhance online discussions?

Effective network discussions rest on the integration of concepts of PLE and ONLE. While most educators currently use an online threaded discussion board in their online instruction, consider also the "network" discussion board. In this way, you can assist learners in shifting their role from online learners to network learners, while you shift your instruction paradigm from online discussions to network discussions.

To achieve effective, interactive network discussions, network discussion tools must provide multiple discussion interfaces (e.g., threaded, nested, and flat); and they must integrate multiple social and networking features (e.g., social tagging, tag or word clouds, RSS, widgets, profiles, and pictures or avatars). With multiple interfaces and multiple social network features, students can be required to engage in active metacognitive and self-regulated learning processes through selecting and applying different and multiple interfaces and social network features to organize, examine, analyze, comprehend, and participate in network discussion or knowledge interaction. Sharing effectively enhances participants' deeper, higher-order, and critical thinking skills. Multidimensional network discussions engage network learners in effective reading (text, auditory, and visual), critical reflecting, displaying (information visualization), and doing (tactile, kinesthetic, and exploratory manipulating information).

To engage students in PLE and ONLE, allow them to select and engage in multiple discussion interfaces and social network features. Network learners define their own organizational scaffolding and learning structures, rather than follow predetermined hierarchical structures.

KEY LINKING THINKING

- Does your discussion board have the features of RSS and e-mail, displaying in threaded and flat format?
- Does your discussion board have a mobile app or RSS app available?
- Does your discussion board allow participants to generate and maintain their digital cognition print?

CHAPTER 11

Tag to Touch Your Community

Have you ever:

- Wished you could access your bookmark from anywhere?
- Found that you could not locate your bookmark?
- Thought about sharing bookmarks with others to build a learning community?

SOCIAL TAGGING LINKAGE DESIGN CONCEPTS

Do you tag your online resources? If yes, do you tag only for yourself? Do you tag and share with others? If yes, do you tag for a community? Do you tag and interlink resources, people, and tools? If yes, do you tag for network learning environments?

Social tagging linkage is a type of distributed cognition that emphasizes social interaction between people, social networking tools, and community to build learning resources and sustain learning environments (cognitive ecosystems). Social tagging describes a network or architecture system that interlinks resources, people, and tools to collaboratively build network learning environments. Social tagging linkage is not simply a mechanism, nor does it merely involve assigning keywords to learning resources. Although tagging is an individual cognitive process, it can help create a dynamic, social, and cognitive ecosystem.

Social tagging linkage is neither a natural nor an automatic process. By integrating social tagging architecture into your learning environments, you and your students can build a community that learns together, as members store, organize, examine, share, observe tag patterns of learning resources,

Figure 11.1   Social Tagging Architecture for a Master's Program

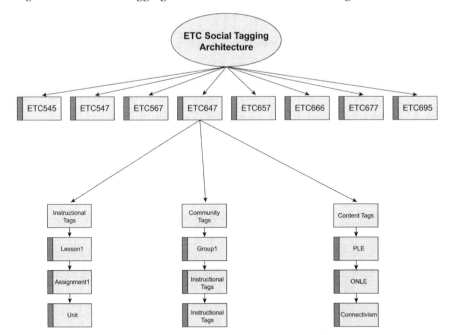

network with other people, and interlink tools. To be successful with social tagging linkage, you first need to build an effective social tagging scheme.

As mentioned, social tagging linkage is more than a tool. It is a structure that uses architecturally designed social and collaborative tagging to link people, content, and tools (see Figure 11.1).

Social tagging, also referred to as collaborative tagging, requires users to apply different mental models to organize and share resources. Most online users are not in the habit of assigning tags. Perhaps they assign one or a few tags to resources, but this is the exception rather than the rule. This is because tagging requires a different cognition process from that required in hierarchical organizations (Tu et al., 2012). The architecture of tagging organization is a flat format, which is generally displayed and organized alphabetically or chronologically. Traditionally, people have organized resources according to a hierarchical format, such as in a folder system based in the Internet browser. Hierarchical function defines a single relation between resource and folder; one resource belongs to one folder only. In contrast, the flat structure tag format allows one resource to be associated with multiple tags.

Tagging allows learners to analyze their distributed learning resources and sum up their distinctiveness in keywords that embody the information.

This approach externalizes the knowledge structures contributed by multiple individuals. Learners exemplify the importance of metadata; so social tagging engages learners in new ways to find and identify network resources, which involves the fundamental skills of analysis, contextualization, conceptualization, self-organization, social sharing, and social networking. By attaching tags to resources, people, and tools in the community, human knowledge and cognition become distributed. Tags may function like keywords; however, they also represent a kind of social annotation; therefore, tags verify community properties. Social tagging illustrates how community cognition moves through community members.

Tagging can be taken to higher levels; by emphasizing individuals and their environments, social tagging becomes an approach for designing social aspects of cognition. Social tagging linkage provides you and your students with an innovative way to organize and reorganize networked learning resources, so they can be shared with communities and collaborative groups. Social tagging linkage activities are collaborative, organized, shared, and practical, and therefore are effective instructional strategies.

Digital literacy is critical to social tagging linkage. Siemens and Cormier (2009) argue that social media are not inherently social. Media are social only when an individual can perceive their use to connect and interact with others. Learners must engage in socially interactive activities to make social media interactive and social. So social tagging linkage may be seen as an individual cognitive process; however, many educators don't know how to assign tags for organizing interlinking, or sharing.

Most people identify and use online resources without organizing them and without sharing them through tags. In fact, many consider using online resources only for personal use. Their tagging behaviors lack "social" and "collaborative" aspects and do not result in effective sharing and social knowledge organization.

To build truly effective network learning environments, network educators and students must also build their social tagging linkage skills. Without effective tags, Web 2.0 tools are simply raw, personal collections of learning resources. Effective strategies for online learners cause learners to contemplate and effectively tag resources for organizing and sharing. With competent social tagging skills, students can assign rich, community-connected tags to resources used in collaborative projects, groups, or classes; and they become involved in an ever-shifting blend of individualization and community activity. In this chapter, you'll learn how to apply an effective social tagging scheme, implement social tagging instructional strategies, and create social tagging linkage designs.

SOCIAL TAGGING DESIGN GUIDELINES

A social tagging scheme is the method used to characterize how knowledge structures could arise and be meaningful to other individuals. The scheme involves a set of systematic methods, skills, and strategies intended to help learners organize and share resources. There are two types of social tagging schemes: "*Organization Stratum* and *Sharing Stratum*. Organization stratum tagging strategies utilize a different type of tags that embody human knowledge and cognition, while sharing stratum uses collaborative tags to share resources with different functions of communities in network environments" (Tu et al, 2012, p. 13).

To Select Social Tagging Tools

Many Web 2.0 tools, such as Delicious, blogs, wikis, network forums, Twitter, Diigo, and Flickr, feature tag fields that allow users to assign tags to organize and link content. They all share similar tagging features (users create/manage tags; searchable; RSS feeds or tag clouds), so they are generally compatible with one another and can be interlinked seamlessly.

To Organize Social Tagging Architecture

There are four types of tags in the organization stratum tagging scheme that you should develop as an educator: community tags, content tags, instructional activity tags, and private tags. When tagging, consider which of the four types of tags should be applied to resources to best embody knowledge and cognition.

Community Tags

The function of community tags is to share learning resources with a specific community. Community tags are critical to community building. Before effective sharing can occur, you need to plan your social tagging architecture strategy and determine appropriate and unique community tags for different levels of communities. The sizes or levels of communities may range from a small group of people to institutional levels. Examples include project or taskforce groups, class groups, classes, programs, and entire organizations. Community tags must be specific, so learning resources can be shared effectively and precisely. If a community tag is not specific, a second community tag can be added to make it distinct (see Table 11.1).

For example, within a course, users may apply "Group1" as a community tag in conjunction with the course number, "EDUC2005." Generally, tags are not case sensitive, but with community tags, keep the case consistent to avoid confusion. To effectively use community tags, groups and communities should define, publish, and communicate their community tags and tag definitions on a log.

Table 11.1 Examples of Community Tags in Various Levels

Communities	Tags
Institutions, Schools, School Districts	NAU (Northern Arizona University) KMMHS (Karen M. Murphy High School)
Program, Department, Center, College	NAUCOE (College of Education, Northern Arizona University) ETCNAU (Educational Technology, Northern Arizona University)
Class	EDUC2005 (Course Number) BUS300 (Business 300)
Class Groups	Group1; Team1 EDU305Group1; EDUC Group1
Project or Taskforce Groups	TechTC (Technology Taskforce Committee) EmTP (Emerging Technology Project)

Content Tags

Content tags label topics extracted from web documents. The representations and interpretations of these tags allow authors and other users to predict contents of different documents efficiently. When applying content tags, keep the following in mind:

- Apply multiple content tags to summarize the content.
- The more content tags there are, the easier the retrieval later.
- The more relevant the content tags, the better the representations and interpretations of the contents are, even without reviewing original tagged web documents.

Instructional Activity Tags

Instructional activity tags are applied to organize network instructional activities, such as instructional units, readings, and assignments. For example, tags could be: Assignment1; Module1; Lesson2; Lesson1RequiredReadings; FinalProject, Spring 2010 (Spr10), and so on. Combining instructional activities tags with community tags allows for easier retrieval of resources.

Private Tags

Private tags refer to tags with an attached personal meaning. Many social tools allow users to keep their resources private. This allows for maintenance of privacy regarding the content and the thoughts (tags) applied to assigned resources. A resource that is saved as private cannot be seen by anyone else. Sometimes you might want to share your private resources but still maintain a degree of privacy. You may want to apply evaluative tags to organize your reflections—for example, ratings of and opinions about learning resources.

Is it possible to have shared resources and to attach personal and private tags that allow users to manage their shared bookmark resources? Yes; the answer is to use public private tags. Applying the tags that have specific meanings only to the owners in public, such as EEE, A1B2C3, and AABD, permits these public tags to be identified only by the owner. These public private tags may contain private information such as ratings and critiques of resources, as well as for personal organization purposes. The meanings of these tags will be difficult if not impossible for others to decode. Although they seem to be "selfish" tags because they do not contribute to social sharing, they empower users to be able to manage personal and private resources in public.

Ask your students to develop specific public private resource tags for their own personal use; that way, they can view their private tags in public and still maintain a certain privacy. It is highly recommended that you keep a log for these public private tags with definitions for each one, insuring that you do not forget their meanings and that they are consistent.

To Share and Collaborate on Social Tagging Architecture

Sharing stratum tagging strategies offer a second dimension to a social tagging scheme that focuses on its sharing and collaborative functions, while organization stratum tagging strategies focus on organizing with different types of tags.

The value of social tagging lies in applying tags to resources in an effort to interact with others to build collaborative knowledge and cognitions in learning communities. There are four different categories of learning communities (Carotenuto et al., 1999), all of which benefit from using tags to share and collaborate on resources: communities of interest, communities of purpose, communities of passion, and communities of practice.

Members in communities of interest "share common backgrounds and interests," which are more broadly focused and tend to be general interests. Members of communities of purpose "share a common desire to focus on specific interests of organizations and groups." Participants in communities of passion focus on "a specific interest to the point of becoming passionate advocates." Members of communities of practice (CoP) are focused on "a common set of activities or practices, and share common or related professional responsibilities or activities. A CoP is considered by educators to be a learning community with online learning as its ultimate goal" (Tu, Blocher, and Roberts,

2008, p. 264). To build a CoP, learners must first engage in building communities of interest, purpose, and passion, because these three elements are the foundation of CoP.

Understanding the different functions of these communities helps learners understand how, what, and why members share and collaborate with learning resources in different communities. In social learning environments, learners engage in different levels of sharing and collaborative activities with various communities. Don't assume that all learners in a community have the same needs in sharing resources, even though the ultimate goal is considered to be the formation of a CoP.

In Table 11.2, the comparison between organization stratum and sharing stratum tagging strategies is displayed, in support of the understanding of effective social tagging. One tag is related to the association of multiple strata.

When preparing a tag to "share," consider which of these four different tagging communities it relates to, and apply only relevant tags. Generally, you should apply multiple tags for each resource. Applying more tags is more effective in creating learning community resources and for knowledge building (see Table 11.3).

Community of Interest (CoI)

Sharing within a CoI involves sharing general interests with a larger group of people by applying individual and separate content tags. This type of community is generally not clearly defined and is more like the general public. The words in your tags should remain separate, as in "Online Collaborative Learning Community, Social Network." With this strategy, each word in the tag has its own meaning, and you can generate broader and multiple meanings with different word combinations, as in "Online Social Learning Community," "Online Social Network," "Network Community," "Online Learning," and so on. Generating broader meanings for the general public doesn't require specific knowledge in content domain.

The advantage of CoI tags is that they make it easy for the author and the general public to retrieve resources—as long as you know and remember one of the tags. Different word combinations may generate meanings for tags that may not have originally been intended. Additionally, it is very easy for community members to locate and retrieve information, because community members can search one or more assigned tags, even though they are not in a logical sequence, allowing the resource to be easily located. For example, you might search for "learning distance" instead of "distance learning." The disadvantages are that CoI tags generate fairly broad meanings. If a community member has specific types of resources in mind, simply searching one or more assigned words may result in an unmanageably large number of resources.

Table 11.2 Comparisons of Organization Stratum and Sharing Stratum

Tags	Social Bookmarking	Folksonomy	Online Learning	NAU	ETC647	Team1	A2B3C1
Organization Stratum	Content Tags			Community tags		Instructional Activity Tags	Private Tags
Sharing Stratum	Community of Interest		Community of Purposes		Community of Practices		N/A
	Community of Passion (# of tags applied)						

Table 11.3   Comparison of Tag to Share for Different Communities

Category	Descriptions	Coding Criteria	Example Tags
Community of Interest	Share common backgrounds/ interests; more diffuse focus.	Individual/ separate tags	Social Bookmarking
Community of Purpose	Share a common desire to focus on specific interests of organizations/ groups as a whole.	Conjugated or compound tag institution; Organizations	Socialbookmarking MountainViewHS
Community of Passion	Focus on a specific interest to the point of becoming passionate advocates.	# of tags applied	Count the # of tags used for each bookmark
Community of Practice	Tight focus on a common set of activities or practices. Share common or related professional responsibilities or activities.	Share with specific persons or smaller group of people	For:JoeSmith; Group1; Team1; GroupProject; ETC647

Community of Purpose (CoPur)

A CoPur shares more specific interests based on content and community tags. The strategy here is to apply compound words or unique community words as tags; for example, "OnlineLearning," "CollaborativeCommunity," "MountainViewHS," or "MVHS." These have more specific meanings than single, separated word tags.

The advantage of CoPur tags is that more precise meanings are assigned to the resources, so retrieval of results is easier. Combined tag meanings have specific meanings. For example, "OnlineLearning" and "Collaborative-Community" retain a similar and specific meaning to "OnlineCollaborative-LearningCommunity." The disadvantages of applying compound-word tags are the requirements that community members must have knowledge of what compound words to search or remember what compound words are used in order to locate and retrieve specific resources.

When tagging resources, it's easy to apply different tags for the same meaning. Those who join the community later may not know either of the interchangeable, compound tags. For example, if you use "DistanceEducation" interchangeably with "DistanceLearning" at the time the resource was tagged, you will have some inconsistency and possibly some confusion. Community members would have to remember two specific, compound tags and apply both to retrieve the needed resource. The solution for this situation would be "redundancy tagging," applying all possible compound-word tags, particularly when interchangeable meanings may be applied.

Community of Passion (CoPas)

A CoPas actively shares resources based on the number of tags applied to each resource. The more tags are used, the easier to retrieve for others, and the more contributions to the community. The numbers of single-word and/or compound-word tags applied reflect the level of the community of passion. The more tags applied, the greater the passion toward communities. How many tags should be assigned to each resource? There is no standard answer to that. However, generally speaking, if you follow the organization stratum tagging strategy, one tag for each of the four types of tags, then a minimum of four tags is required. Instruct students to apply at least two tags for each tag type. In other words, at least eight tags should be applied to each resource.

According to studies on Delicious, the general public applied an average of only 3.16 tags to each resource (Wetzker, Zimmermann, and Bauckhage, 2008). It is highly recommended that community members first consider what organization stratum tags (community, content, instructional activity, and private tags) should be assigned and what sharing stratum tags should be applied for different functions of communities. For example, to tag the article "Gamification in Education: What, How, Why Bother? (Lee and Hammer, 2011)," we may tag it with tags Gamification and Education; however, to achieve better CoPas, we may provide more tags: Gamification, Education, Peer-Review Journal Article, Columbia University, Cognitive Benefits, Social Benefits, Emotional Benefits. The later tags provide more information to the article, which supports CoPas. It is easier for others to locate this article by searching different tags.

Community of Practice (CoP)

A CoP shares resources within fairly focused groups by assigning community and instructional activity tags. Members in a CoP are bonded with specific interests, tasks, and practices. CoI and CoPur tags reflect certain interests and content areas. CoP tags could be for specific persons (JoeSmith, to: JoeSmith), groups of people with specific goals and tasks to achieve (GrantReviewCommunittee or GRC; Group1), or specific courses (ETC647; ED550). It is vital that the community members agree about which tags should be applied for their shared purposes. For example, they might choose between Grant Review Community, GrantReviewCommunity, or GRC.

Groups and communities (such as course, program, or school levels) should develop and publish their CoP tag Scheme, so community members (teachers, students, staff, administrators, and parents and any other relevant stakeholders) know it and are able to assign appropriate CoP tags as needed. Without correct or unique CoP tags, the resources cannot be correctly shared and retrieved. Community members should apply CoP tags in combination with content tags (CoI and CoPur tags) to permit more in-depth sharing of knowledge. Any additional content tags would provide supplementary values for members to understand shared resources. CoP should avoid changing tags, as it creates confusion. If it is necessary to change a tag, the community should notify all members and instruct them to update their CoP tags.

Tag Cleanup

As you apply more tags, remember to review, clean, revise, and consolidate your social tagging architectures regularly, so resources and tags remain effective for personal and community collaboration. Vocabulary problems lead to incoherent tags. People generally do not assign tags consistently for interchangeable tags, plural-singular terms, single-compound tags, acronyms, hyphenated words, incomplete, or misspelled words. Community members also should review and update their tags regularly to keep the tagging scheme consistent, just as institutions, schools, programs, courses, and teachers must regularly review their social tagging architectures.

Typically, Web 2.0 tools with tagging features allow users to edit the tags individually or in batches. It is useful to maintain a tag definition log as a personal reference and a reference for community members. Institutions should publish their social tagging architectures to communicate tag definitions and schemes. In your course setting, remind students to clean up their tags regularly. In fact, tag cleanup could be integrated into your instructional activities. Tag clouds are an effective way to examine any incoherent tags by observing the visual depictions of user-generated tags. Tag cloud techniques are discussed later in this chapter.

SOCIAL TAGGING LINKAGE ACTIVITY DESIGNS

To Create Social Tagging Activities

- Engaging learners in social tagging activities in online learning instructions.
- Encouraging students to share and collaborate with social tagging resources.
- Asking students to build a social tagging architecture for their learning community.
- Engaging learners in creating and integrating tag clouds instructions.

SOCIAL TAGGING LINKAGE DESIGNS

Social and network linkage designs for tagging involve applying social tagging to link multiple tools, people, and resources. InfoViz and RSS linkages can enhance learning resources organization, while you and your students can use social network linkage to explore the social networks of other community members and enrich shared resources.

- *Personal portal linkage*: Many tools with social tagging features—such as Delicious, Diigo, or Flickr—can be added to personal learning portals. Linking the tools with social tagging features to your (or your students') personal portal makes personal learning more effective. You (or your students) do not need to visit every single tool to view social tagging resources.
- *RSS linkage*: RSS linkage is another way to link tools and resources and strengthen social tagging linkage. Subscribing to RSS allows users to update with newly shared resources. Community members can constantly add new resources with tags. Of course, not all members' resources will interest the other members. Generally, there are just certain types of resource tags each member will be interested in. RSS allows you to subscribe to selective tags from members' resources. Ask your students to subscribe to specific content tags based on the instructional unit topic, lessons, or modules. That way, students do not need to remember to constantly look for content resources. If they read their RSS subscriptions regularly, they will be automatically updated.

  RSS linkage can also interlink multiple tools. Community members tag resources on multiple tools, but it is tedious to visit multiple tools to review shared resources. Even with RSS subscriptions, reviewing large numbers of resources on multiple tools in multiple locations becomes awkward and time-consuming. Generally, with RSS, you can subscribe to the web browser such as Firefox or Internet Explorer. If you have a large number of RSS subscriptions, use your RSS organizer to organize large amounts of live feed resources. Several RSS organizers are available, such as Google Reader (http://www.google.com/reader) or Microsoft Outlook RSS reader.
- *Widget linkage*: You can embed social tagging tools into most webpages via widget linkage. That way, social tagging resources can be displayed on the webpage as live and interactive content, without your having to visit original social tagging tools. Examples of social tagging resources include Diigo's group widget, Delicious's widget, and Delicious's widget for blogs. You can also link social tagging to a webpage by integrating RSS feed with social tagging.

- *Social network linkage*: The power of social tagging involves more than just organizing and sharing resources. Social networking linkage allows expansion of networked learning resources. Web 2.0 tools generally contain social networking features that allow users to network with other users by becoming friends, fans, or followers. When socially networked, users are granted privileges to view their friends' tagging resources and their social networks. By viewing their friends' networks, they can identify more people with the same or similar interests and expand their learning network. Require students and learning community members to network with others. By becoming friends, fans, and followers, group and community members will strengthen their social tagging linkage powers.

Here are a few strategies you can use to engage students or community members in active social networking.

- Ask them to become friends, fans, and followers of each other and explore the social networks of their friends.
- Encourage them to explore the social networks of other members.
- Suggest that they apply InfoViz tools to explore their social network and the social networks of others. For example, Delicious Network Explorer (http: //www.twoantennas.com/projects/delicious -network-explorer/) is an effective tool to analyze your own network and that of your friends. Through the visual effect, you can also easily locate people who have similar interests. These visual network exploring tools offer opportunities for visualizing social networks that traditional friend-listing format cannot offer.
- Apply any additional tools, such as Facebook, Ning, or Friend Wheel applications, to strengthen the social network of members (https://www.facebook.com/pages/Friend-Wheel/85922088935). Friend Wheel for Facebook can be applied to obtain a visual representation of your Facebook social network.
- *Mobile linkage*: Many Web 2.0 tools with social tagging features have mobile apps. Linking social tagging features to mobile devices expands social tagging abilities to anywhere and any time. It empowers students to tag and share resources from their mobile devices, and these shared tagged resources are more meaningful. For example, students could use a mobile phone camera to take photos and upload them from the mobile phone and tag them to share with the target audiences. These tags share meaningful resources that are more difficult for desktop or laptop computers to achieve. This activity is particularly useful when the students are on a field trip. When they observe something they would like to record, taking

a picture or recording a video is often more effective than taking notes. With relevant tags, it will be easier for them to search, retrieve, and share after the field trip.

- *InfoViz linkage*: Information visualization linkage is an effective way to organize your tags. A tag cloud is a visual depiction of user-generated tags. Tag clouds are a visual representation of tags or keywords assigned by users. They can be used to understand, scan, explore, and organize tag context and resource meanings. The larger the tag font size, the more frequently used the tags are. Review your tag cloud to determine whether it accurately reflects your thinking. Study your community tag clouds to obtain overall understanding of learning resources. Additionally, tag clouds allow users to draw inferences from the relationships of tags by examining clusters of tags. In fact, reviewing the tag clouds of individuals or the one produced by a community is an effective way to understand the interests and thinking of that person and the collaborative knowledge of a community.

Tags are hyperlinks to a collection of items associated with that tag. Tag clouds can be dynamically or manually generated. Dynamic tag clouds reflect current assigned tags in real time, while static tag clouds are a snapshot of assigned tags. Diigo's tag clouds (http://www.diigo.com/cloud/) are an example of dynamic clouds that display popular tags in real time. Wordle (http://www.wordle.net/) is a tool for generating clouds manually. Users copy and paste tags to generate static tag clouds. Both dynamic and static tag clouds can be useful, and they maintain different distributed social context values. As an instructor, you can apply dynamic tag clouds to better understand the current social tagging in context and to monitor the real-time emerging and evolving of distributed resources. Static tag clouds provide the value of a snapshot of resources. This is a great way to observe different stages of learning resources in context; it is particularly helpful to compare vertical and horizontal tags. Vertically, different static tag clouds reveal different stages of resource contexts for exploring hidden patterns in individual or community levels. Horizontally, different static tag clouds from different communities allow you to compare and contrast cognition and knowledge of different communities, or even the cognition and knowledge of specific individuals compared to the rest of the community. For example, students can compare their own tag clouds to the groups' or class's tag clouds to enhance their metacognition. By examining the tag clouds, the students can see the frequently used tags in social bookmarking resources. These tags represent more social bookmarked resources. By comparing personal tag clouds to the groups' or class's tag clouds, the students would gain a better idea of what resources they lack or that they contribute more to the community. In such metacognitive enhancement, the students can organize, manage, and update their tagged resources to align and coordinate with the community shared resources.

LEARNING ACTIVITY:
SOCIAL TAGGING TO SUPPORT
NETWORK LEARNING COMMUNITY

Purpose: To integrate social tagging design to enhance network learning instructions

Instructions: This social tagging instructional activity engages students in active learning and collaboration. You can embed and infuse social tagging activities into existing instructional learning activities, and build innovative social tagging activities, such as readings, assignments, projects, exercises, group collaboration, discussions, or learning resource locating, and so on.

Define Course Social Tagging Architectures

Plan, define, and communicate your course's social tagging architectures before any social tagging instructional activities occur; or work with learners to define the effective tagging architectures. The architecture you use should be well thought-out and consistently applied across multiple integrated Web 2.0 tools and instructional activities. Define tags for courses, instructional units, assignments, assigned readings, discussions, and projects. These tags can be combined, hyphenated, or joined together to become unique, to organize, and to share. Below are a few examples:

- Course numbers can be effective tags for courses, because generally they are unique on the web, such as ETC674. If not, try adding the school's acronym, such as JHH (Johnson High School) to the course number, JHHETC647, JHH-ETC647, JHH ETC647.
- For instructional units: Module1, Lesson1, or Unit1 can be added or used.
- For assignments: try Assignment1, A1, or Paper1.
- For assigned Readings: consider M1RR (Module 1 Required Readings) or M1OR (Module1 Optional Readings).
- For discussions: you could use M1D (Module 1 Discussion) or #ETC647M1D for Twitter discussions.
- For Projects: consider FP (Final Project) or P1 (Project 1).
- Combined, hyphenated, or joined tags: "ETC647, M1, Required Readings," "ETC647-M1-Required-Readings," or ETC647M1Required Readings" for ETC647 Module1 Required Readings.

Organized Assigned Readings

You can assign online readings by organizing tags on social bookmarking tools, such as Delicious (http://delicious.com). Apply relevant tags for required readings, optional readings, and resources for instructional units. For example, on Delicious you might have ETC647L1Required (or ETC647, Lesson1, Required) or ETC647L1Optional, ETC647L1 (for resources). Provide a URL that displays a list of required readings; for example, http://delicious.com/ChihTu/ETC647+Lesson1+Required. (With this URL, students can view a list of Lesson 1 required readings that this author has assigned, because the URL points to "ChihTu.") For other resources, ask students to contribute/collaborate on their shared learning resources with the class by using resource tag ETC647 Lesson1, http://delicious.com/tag/ETC647+Lesson1. Students can view this URL for a list of Lesson 1 resources shared by students and instructors because the URL points to "tag" rather than to a specific Delicious user.

Embedded in Existing Course Activities

Social tagging can be easily integrated into existing assignments and activities. Students are generally required to provide sources, references, or bibliographies for their assignments. You can require them to post their sources on Delicious with required tags; for example, http://delicious.com/tag/ETC647 +Assignment4. These types of instructional activities facilitate community-community interaction because the resources of multiple semesters are shared by students. In other words, current students can view assignment resources of previous students. This cross-time interaction and shared resources are valuable for distributed cognition. The course community learns because resources are tagged by students and aggregated from multiple semesters. Digital generations are used to aggregate their network learning content. Students are further empowered by integrating social tagging to organize and share instructional resources. If you wish, you can assign additional instructional activity tags and separate shared resources from different semesters, such as "ETC647, Assignment4, Spring, 2010" or "ETC647, Assignment4, Spr10," and so on.

Build Collaborative Groups and Communities

People frequently attend meetings, conferences, or events together, or work together in groups on certain tasks. Unique and effective tags bond group and community members, and provide a way for them to contribute ideas and resources. Working groups could assign unique tags, such as AAC (Academic Assessment Community); while meetings, conferences, and events could assign AECT2010 (Association for Educational Communication Technology 2010 conference). These tags can be applied to multiple Web 2.0 tools—such as blogs, Twitter, Delicious, Flickr, or wiki—for example, by applying hashtag "#AECT2010" on Twitter for a conference.

Organize Online Discussion Postings

Applying tags to organize network discussion boards is an effective way to support distributed cognition. Research (Schellens et. al., 2009) has concluded that "tagging thinking" instructions significantly enhance the critical thinking process. Most Web 2.0 forum tools feature social tagging fields that allow users to assign tags and summarize their postings. Thus, assigning tags to discussion posts involves students in effective distributed cognition and in coordinating internal and external tagging structures. Consider requiring students to provide both "content" tags and "community" tags. Multiple tags should at least be encouraged. If necessary, you can monitor and assess the message tags on the relevancy to the postings. Convert all posting tags into tag clouds to assist students in gaining a bigger picture of discussion topics.

You can also apply extended tag cloud activities to support discussions. Students frequently engage in more parent-child postings (one-to-one, reading-reply actions) in online discussion boards. They sometimes lack an overall understanding of discussion topics and even deviate from them. Students are rarely asked to summarize and reflect on their own discussion postings. Instead, summarizing tasks falls on the shoulders of discussion moderators or teachers. Generally, Web 2.0 forum tools allow tagging only the initial discussion question and not reply postings. To overcome this barrier, require students to modify the "Subject" field when they reply to postings with relevant tags as keywords. You can then generate tag clouds regularly, such as every other day, or every three to four days, depending on the length of the discussions. In addition, require students to observe and analyze tag clouds before the actual reading of each individual posting to gain an overview of the emergence of the discussion topics. At the end of the discussion activity, instructors ask students to reveal their tag clouds based on the posting tags and compare their individual tag clouds to the overall discussion topic tag clouds. Students can post their reflections on tag cloud comparisons as the final posting to wrap up their discussion experiences.

Conduct Tag Search

Conducting tag search on multiple Web 2.0 tools is an effective way for students to locate relevant learning resources. Ask them to conduct tag search on Web 2.0 tools, such as Delicious, Diigo, Blogs, network forums, or Flickr, to locate learning resources instead of using an Internet search engine, such as Google or Bing. This instructional activity can help students understand the power of social tagging.

Internet search engines organize network information by web server, while web users organize with social tagging. Recent studies (Morrison, 2008) have shown that relevancy and accuracy of tag searches are as effective as Internet search engines. Although social tagging is not a controlled vocabulary, the distributed tags have been shown to converge over time to a stable power, according to the law of distributions. In other words, the power of crowd sources and social content sharing may provide resources to determine accuracy as relevant to professional keyword assigning, such as library catalogue keywords. In fact, if users apply relevant tags to their searches, tag searches on Delicious provide more accurate and precise search results than those from search engines, which return more general results. If you have the knowledge of what relevant tags to search, Delicious can be a more effective way to search. Of course, if you are unclear about what to search, search engines would be the more effective choice.

Tag searches allow you and your students to search familiar tags and narrow them down to reach relevant information. In fact, with community tagging, tag search may generate more social context and richer and more meaningful search results, which search engines lack. Tag search allows users to gain a better understanding of how to locate trustworthy resources that are not available on any search engine. When community members tag more Internet resources, the accuracy and relevancy of tag search may outperform the usual search engines.

LAST WORDS

Social tagging resources can be seen on Delicious in Chapter 1, Table 1.1.

Community memory and knowledge rely on sharing distributed learning environments. It is critical that you and your students have a correct understanding of social tagging, as well as the skills of social tagging linkage.

Social tagging linkage is a new way of contributing, organizing, and sharing collaboratively the mass of information and resources available on network environments. To build effective collaborative and sharing communities demands that students be equipped with social tagging skills. The ability of learners to maneuver within social media does not necessarily mean they are capable of engaging in social collaboration through social media. You must teach learners new digital literacy skills in social tagging to apply social media in constructing effective learning community and community learning. It is your responsibility as an educators to prepare and engage learners to "tag to share," "tag to organize," and "tag to collaborate" by ensuring they possess competent social tagging linkage skills and allowing them to ascertain what to tag for sharing with different community learners collaboratively.

CHAPTER 12

Erase the Invisibility

Have you ever:

- Been overwhelmed by large and complicated online information and data?
- Thought of yourself as a visual learner rather than a verbal learner?
- Thought about integrating visualization to support digital learning?

INFOVIZ LINKAGE DESIGN CONCEPTS

Information visualization (InfoViz), or InfoGraphics, refers to an information design that "uses picture, symbols, colors, and words to communicate ideas, illustrate information, or express relationships visually" (Emerson, 2008, p. 4). Research has concluded that InfoViz supports learning in: problem-solving (Ware, 2004); knowledge acquisition (Keller et. al., 2005); decision making (Chi, 2002; Spencer, 2007); understanding large and otherwise inaccessible amounts of data (Ware, 2004); recognizing unanticipated associations among data (Ware); discovering new explanations (Tufte, 1997); forming hypotheses about observed relationships (Ware); reducing cognitive load (Perkins, 1993); sense making (Chi); and allowing technology to support knowledge co-construction (Perkins). Card, Mackinlay, and Shneiderman (1999) argue that effective InfoViz linkage design includes six aspects:

- Memory and processing capabilities
- Information search paths
- Pattern detection
- Critical information

- Inferences
- Data manipulations

Within this information-overload era, reading every word and visiting every page on a site, or even checking every site available, may not be the most effective ways for students to understand or absorb educational content, instructions, and activities. InfoViz effectively supports both learners and instructors in organizing and personalizing online learning by transforming information into a visual format that enhances learning and teaching. It becomes particularly powerful when learners organize and personalize their learning information into InfoViz format as part of their PLE.

INFOVIZ DESIGN GUIDELINES

To Select InfoViz Linkage Tools and Data

Your first step in InfoViz integration to determine what information should be visualized. When information and instructions are large scale or overwhelming for learners, InfoViz may help. Online discussion postings, course activities and events, and writing assignments can all benefit from an InfoViz approach.

To Organize InfoViz Linkage

InfoViz tools are organizational tools. Selecting the appropriate InfoViz tool to convert and display information into a visual format is critical. Keep in mind that not all visual tools are considered InfoViz tools. Generally, an effective InfoViz tool should be able to (a) organize a large amount of information, (b) feed live information to InfoViz to reflect real-time information, (c) interactively display InfoViz graphics in different viewing formats, and (d) convert original format into more effective visual formats (e.g., from list format to timeline format or from one dimension to multiple dimensions). An InfoViz tool does not necessarily contain *all* of these features but should contain some of them.

When selecting an InfoViz tool for your purposes, consider which features would most improve your instruction. Certainly, a tool that has more features would be more flexible and offer more options, but consider your needs and the needs of your students.

To Share and Collaborate via InfoViz Linkage

When creating an InfoViz linkage, focus on sharing InfoViz with learners and creating collaboration among them and with you. Be sure your network instructions encourage students to create, share, and collaborate with Info-Viz amongst themselves rather than only with you. Allowing them to create, share, and collaborate on InfoViz makes their learning more meaningful, particularly when they generate the data and the information.

To Link Tools to InfoViz Linkage

For optimum learning, be sure to link multiple online and network tools to InfoViz tools. Online learning tools, such as online discussion boards, chat rooms, and instructional calendars, generally have fairly simple and basic features for conducting online learning activities. By linking online learning tools to other network learning tools and InfoViz tools, open network learning becomes more interactive, meaningful, and, productive. For example, you can link online discussion boards to social tagging, tag and word clouds, or instructional calendars to network timeline-based visualization.

INFOVIZ LINKAGE ACTIVITY DESIGNS

To Create InfoViz Activities

- Explain the values of InfoViz to students
- Ask students to create and generate InfoViz documents
- Integrate InfoViz components into existing learning activities, such as online discussions, course calendar, and social networks.

INFOVIZ LINKAGE DESIGNS

Besides connecting InfoViz to tools, people, and resources, you can also apply the linkage design model to other categories. Consider which linkages will best suit your instructional needs, and select those that are most relevant and appropriate.

Below are a few suggestions regarding the application of each linkage to enhance your InfoViz instruction.

- *RSS linkage*: Many InfoViz tools, such as Dipity and Wordle, use RSS to link, organize, and visually present raw data and information.
- *Third-party linkage*: Some Web 2.0 tools, such as blogs and wiki, have word cloud gadgets that can be applied to generate word clouds from groups of words.
- *Social tagging linkage*: Many social tagging tools (e.g., Delicious, Diigo, or Blogger) have tag cloud features that allow users to apply tags to generate tag clouds.
- *Social network linkage*: Some Web 2.0 tools, like Facebook, have apps (e.g., Friend Wheel) and built-in InfoViz tools (e.g., Facebook Timeline for a digital resume).

- *Mobile linkage*: Some InfoViz tools (see http://pinterest.com/jordisancho/mobile-infographics/) are available on mobile devices. Do not forget to check mobile linkage feature when selecting your InfoViz tools.

LEARNING ACTIVITY: APPLY INFOVIZ TO ENHANCE ONLINE DISCUSSIONS

Case I:
Integrating Words and Tag Clouds to Enhance Online Discussions

Purpose:

To integrate InfoViz strategy to facilitate class discussions and foster in participants a deeper understanding.

Instructions:

Using InfoViz can address some of the weaknesses of the threaded online discussion format, such as lack of synthesis of discussions, derailed discussions, fragmented understanding, and loss of sense of original discussion topics.

You can design social tagging activities for online discussions to provide missing context. In fact, social tagging allows users to organize and reorganize the entire discussion message to their desired, personal formats. Schellens et al. (2009) concluded that tagging would, if fact, increase critical thinking.

Wordle is an InfoViz tool, with which users generate tag clouds or word clouds. A tag/word cloud is a visual depiction of user-generated tags or the word content of a site or an article. Tags are usually single words, and they are normally listed alphabetically, with the importance of a tag/word shown by font size or color. User-generated tags are words. Frequently, they are sorted and displayed alphabetically and by the frequency of use represented by different font color or size. Larger font size represents a tag/word used more frequently.

Clouds have been the subject of research in several usability studies. Lohmann, Ziegler, and Tetzlaff (2009) concluded that tag/word clouds support data analysis in that large tags attract more attention; users can scan tags rather than read them; tags in the middle of the cloud attract more attention; the upper-left quadrant receives more attention; and tag clouds support exploration.

Both dynamic and static tag/word clouds offer distributed social context value, although of different types. You can apply dynamic tag/word clouds to understand up-to-date social tagging among your students and monitor the real-time evolution of online discussions; while static tag/word clouds provide a snapshot of the discussion. This is a great way to observe and contextualize different stages of online discussion; it is particularly effective when you compare vertical and horizontal orientations. When observed vertically, static tag/word clouds reveal different stages of online discussions and allow you to explore patterns at individual or community levels. When you observe tags horizontally, static tag/word clouds from different communities allow you to compare and contrast the knowledge of different communities or of specific individuals compared to the rest of the community.

Here are the instructions you can apply:

- Review your existing online discussion activities.
- Ask students to follow and provide tags for each of their postings in the "Subject" field. If necessary, explain how to insert tags in that field. When you initiate a discussion thread, or reply to a discussion message, you can type in the subject field or change it in accordance with your participation. These tags function like keywords for their posting and should summarize their posting. Be sure to instruct students to do this; otherwise the tag clouds will not aptly represent the discussion.
- Use Wordle to generate tag and word clouds regularly to put student discussions into context.
  - To generate tag clouds:
    - Copy and paste all provided tags from the subject fields to Wordle.
    - Generate the tag cloud by clicking "Generate" or "Go."
    - Share the tag cloud with the students in the discussion board, and remind them that these are to help them understand the discussion development.
  - To generate word clouds
    - Copy and paste the entire posting thread (subject field and body texts of postings) to Wordle.
    - Generate the word cloud by clicking "Generate" or "Go."
    - Share the word cloud with the students in the discussion board, and remind them that these are to help them understand the discussion development.

FAQS

Q: How frequently should I generate tag/word clouds?
A: If your online discussion is running on a weekly cycle, generating two tag/word clouds per week is necessary (every three to four days). If your online discussions are very active, consider generating tag/word clouds more often.

Q: How many tags should I require students to provide?
A: The more the better, As long as the provided tags adequately reflect the postings.

Q: How do I modify the appearance of word tags and word clouds to ensure they all have the same font, layout, and colors?
A: Remove standardized words, such as "the," "a," "of," and "to," so clouds more accurately reflect the actual postings. This is particularly critical to the word "clouds," since many such words are copied and they may distract from that word.

- Remove these words: "Print," "Subject," "Author," "Topic," "Date," "Reply," "Forward."
- Right mouse-click the word Remove

If you have student moderators for your online discussion activities, consider having them generate the tag/word clouds. This process offers students additional learning opportunities, and they will have better understanding of the value of applying tag and word clouds to support online discussions.

Ask each student to generate her own tag and word clouds from her own postings. Compare her tag and word clouds to the groups' or class's tag clouds to enhance their metacognition.

If you have multiple discussion threads, consider generating and comparing different sets of tag and word clouds for each discussion thread.

- Advise students to review the generated tag and word clouds before they read every posting to obtain an overall understanding of the discussion. This allows them to better grasp the key discussion points and follow the development of the topics.
- Either you or your student discussion moderator should take the leadership to reflect on the generated tag and word clouds. Share your observations on tag and word clouds. Advise students what has been discussed, whether the discussion stayed on track, and how it developed and evolved.
- As an instructor, you can compare and contrast different tag and word clouds to ensure the discussion thread stays on track and catch it before it derails from the original topic.

TIPS

Some discussion board tools, such as Nabble, have RSS feed features, which allow users to generate live and dynamic word clouds on Wordle.

Case II:
Visualizing Course Activities

Purpose:

To visualize course activities (e.g., calendar, announcement, social bookmarks, resources, blog) on a timeline format.

Instructions:

Generally, course activities and resources are displayed chronologically or in other formats that may not be intuitive to some learners. Additionally, students are often required to visit multiple sites to obtain course instructions.

Dipity, a timeline-based tool, displays multiple instructional activities and resources from multiple sites in a timeline format.

- Create your Dipity account.
- Create a timeline for your course or instructional unit.
- Add events and resources to the timeline.
  - Course calendar
    - If you use Google Calendar or any calendar that has an RSS feed feature, you can obtain the calendar RSS feed and add it to the Dipity timeline.
  - Announcements
    - If you use Twitter as your course announcement tool, you can add it to your Dipity timeline.
  - Social bookmark
    - If you use Delicious or any other social tagging tool to share social bookmarks, you can add social bookmark resources to the Dipity timeline event.
  - Others: You can also add many other resources to the timeline:
    - Photo: Flickr, Picasa
    - Video: YouTube, Vimeo
    - Blog: Blogger, WordPress, Tumblr
    - Music: Last.fm, Pandora
    - Others: Yelp, Digg, Delicious, RSS feeds
- You can embed the Dipity timeline in your course website or syllabus. To do this:
  - Visit the timeline.
  - Select "Embed" from the upper-right corner of the timeline.
  - Copy and paste the embed code into the course website.

Case III:
Integrating Word Clouds to Improve Writing Assignments

Purpose:

To use InfoViz to improve students' writing.

Instructions:

While writing a paper, students frequently overlook their main ideas or key points, or fail to use consistent language. Applying Wordle's word cloud to examine and reflect on students' writing can assist them in observing the patterns and key points of their paper.

- Choose a specific writing assignment. This activity is more effective with longer papers.
- Ask students to copy and paste the draft of their paper into Wordle.
- Tell students to examine the word clouds that are created and observe whether the word cloud represents their paper in these areas: overall ideas, key arguments, overused words and phrases, and inconsistent word choices and phrases.

- To ensure students actually have done this activity, you can require them to include their word clouds in the paper, to provide their reflections on it, and to address how they may have used word clouds to improve their writing.
- Encourage students to apply multiple word clouds in enhancing their writing assignments rather than just one.

LAST WORDS

Social tagging resources can be seen on Delicious in chapter 1, Table 1.1. Many students are visual learners. They may not be familiar with InfoViz instructional activities because they are accustomed to text-based online learning instructions, but InfoViz is a great way to accommodate visual learners. Below are a few tips to help you to integrate InfoViz effectively.

- Explain InfoViz and how you will use it before the course starts.
- Engage students in a warm-up discussion session in which they use InfoViz before the actual graded discussion session starts.
- Generate tag and word clouds more frequently when discussions become extremely active.
- Involve students in peer moderation and generating tag and word clouds for discussions, so they better appreciate the value of InfoViz tools.
- When sharing clouds, remind students how to apply InfoViz's six aspects (memory and processing capabilities, information search paths, pattern detection, critical information, inferences, and data manipulations) to analyze the clouds and InfoViz. (See Chapter 12.)
- Encourage students to observe and analyze InfoViz development and evolution over time.
- Explain that they should still read each discussion posting. Observing clouds is not a substitute for reading postings.
- Remind students that they should observe and analyze clouds first, then read postings.

CHAPTER 13

Go Beyond Texts

Have you ever:

- Thought about using an online discussion board for more than just online discussions?
- Considered adding audio and video components to your online discussions?
- Wondered if you could participate in online discussions via your mobile phone or other tools?

MULTIMODALITY REPRESENTATION DESIGN CONCEPTS

When you think of online learning activities, what probably comes to mind first is using computers to participate in text-based online learning. In fact, your online learning activities are not limited to text-based communication, to computers, nor to online discussions. Instead, they can be implemented as multimodality representations (MMR). The media can be text, audio, video, or all three. The devices can be computers, telephones, tablets, or smartphones. The tools can be VoiceThread, Vialogues, or Twitter. Activities can involve online discussions, storytelling, language learning, drama, and more.

With the features of multimodalities representation, open network learning can become more creative and diversified and move beyond desktop computers to meet learners' personal needs, as well as reflect social and cultural contexts. It is among your responsibilities to ensure that the integrated online instructions are interactive and to foster and facilitate learners' creativity and learning needs.

MULTIMODALITY REPRESENTATION DESIGN GUIDELINES

To Select MMR

To design an effective MMR, it is critical to select appropriate media, devices, tools, and activities. For the media, you can choose from text, audio, video, and any combination of them. With devices, your choice is between computers, telephones, tablets, and smartphones. As tools, consider Voice Thread, Vialogues, or Twitter. And for your activities, you can include online discussions, storytelling, language learning, or drama learning.

You need not predetermine all of the features of your MMR when you first design it; however, do keep in mind that if a tool or device has more features than the others, it will be more flexible and better help you design an effective MMR.

To Organize MMR

Different devices and tools offer different accessing and organization features. While planning your MMR, examine the available features, such as personal portal, widget, RSS, social tagging, social network, mobile, and InfoViz.

To Share and Collaborate on MMR

Regardless of which learning activities are integrated, sharing and collaborating on MMR activities are vital to achieving an optimum learning community. However, you should also consider how private or public your MMR needs to be. This will depend on learning contexts that you and your students should be aware of and how much students would like sharing their MMR instructions.

To Link Tools to MMR

MMR instructions should include directions for linking different tools and devices. MMR has flexible and linkable features; therefore, multiple tools and devices, such as computers and mobile devices, can link MMR activities. Many MMR tools can be accessed on telephones, tablets, cellular phones, and smartphones in addition to computers. For example, many tools have mobile apps available for mobile devices to access MMR content and resources.

MMR ACTIVITY DESIGNS

To Create MMR Activities

- Participatory web activities, such as online discussion and blogging
- User-generated content (UGC) activities, such as creating learning content for other learners
- Community-community interactive activities, such as collaborations with previous, existing, and future learning community
- Social content sharing activities, such as language learning
- Social networking activities, such as social networking with other learners
- Mobile learning activities, such as participating in the course via mobile devices

LINKAGE DESIGNS FOR MMR

Besides connecting tools, people, and resources, linkage design models can also help you design a more effective and comprehensive ONLE. Use each linkage model as a guide to design effective RSS activities. It is not necessary that you integrate all linkages from the linkage design model, but consider all of them and determine which linkages might be the most effective additions to your instruction.

- *Personal portal linkage*: Link tools and devices to personal portal, such as iGoogle or smartphone.
- *RSS linkage*: Identify RSS availability on tools.
- *Widget linkage*: Link tools via embedded gadget to websites or webpages.
- *Social tagging linkage*: Use social tagging feature to link the tools and content.
- *Social network linkage*: Network learners who have similar interests.
- *Mobile linkage*: Link media, tools, and activities to mobile learning, so learners can engage in MMR instructions anywhere and any time.
- *InfoViz linkage*: Link MMR to visual and graphical presentation to view different aspects of MMR.

LEARNING ACTIVITY:
MULTIMODALITY ONLINE DISCUSSIONS

Purpose: To engage learners in multimedia and multidevice online discussion activities.

In this Learning Activity, you will apply VoiceThread to support online discussions. VoiceThread is a collaborative, multimedia slideshow that holds images, documents, and video, and allows learners to navigate slides and leave their comments via five media: text, voice (microphone or telephone), audio files, and video.

Instructions:
- Create your VoiceThread account, and have students create their own accounts.
- Post a discussion topic:
  - The discussion topic can be posted in text format or other formats, such as audio, video, image, document, or a URL for a webpage.
- Encourage students to use different media to post and share their comments, such as text, recorded audio, or recorded video.
- Post comments with mobile devices using VoiceThread Mobile:
  - VoiceThread Mobile allows students to access and post their content and comment via mobile devices, such as iPhone, iPad, and iPod Touch.
  - With mobile devices, students can capture images from the phone camera or upload from the phone's picture library.
  - Other students can comment and annotate while one student narrates.
  - Learners can receive notification for new comments on VoiceThread App.
- Phone commenting (a paid feature):
  - Visit VoiceThread topic.
  - Click "Comments" button.
  - Select the telephone icon.
  - Follow the audio prompt.
- Embed VoiceThread to a webpage:
  - Visit the VoiceThread topic.
  - Click "Menu" on the upper left.
  - Click "Embed."
  - Copy "Embed Code."
  - Paste code to the webpage.

LAST WORDS

Social tagging resources can be seen on Delicious in chapter 1, Table 1.1.

MMR is a powerful way to engage learners in active learning. Don't limit your MMR design to online discussion activities or the VoiceThread tool. Digital storytelling, language learning, or drama learning can also be used effectively. Vialogues, blogs, Twitter, or Facebook can help you achieve effective MMR instruction as well. Remember, many MMR tools allow students to comment by using multimedia formats and different devices, such as mobile devices.

PART VI

COMPREHENSIVE INTEGRATION

Part VI presents a full-scale PLE and ONLE integration without using an LMS and advance PLE and ONLE to another level of learning, global digital citizenship.

CHAPTER 14

Innovate to Create

Have you ever:

- Considered designing and teaching online instructions without integrating a traditional learning management system?
- Wondered how you might design and teach online without purchasing any online tools?
- Wanted to integrate online tools that your students have access to and are fairly familiar with, but wondered how it could be done?

COMPREHENSIVE LINKAGE DESIGN CONCEPTS

In previous chapters, you learned about various linkage designs and network tools to support PLE and ONLE. But is it possible to deliver entire online instructions without using LMS or paid tools at all? The answer is yes. This concept, which you'll learn more about in this section, takes PLE and ONLE to a full and comprehensive scale. In each previous chapter, topics were covered in sections for smaller integration design. In this chapter, you will find out how to connect different linkage designs and multiple network tools to create a fully functioning ONLE and to support PLE.

For an effective PLE and ONLE, you need to integrate a full range of linkage design model and a wide range of ONLE instructional strategies: UGC; community-community interaction; aggregations; mash-ups; social content sharing; remix content; RSS; participatory web; social tagging; social networking; mobile learning; and cloud computing. These strategies are essential features to integrate into your ONLE in order to fully achieve the functions of learning management, communication, content creation, collaboration, distributed resources, and social networking.

COMPREHENSIVE LINKAGE DESIGN GUIDELINES

To Select Effective Network Tools for ONLE and PLE

First, select your network tools—this is critical. Although a tool itself may or may not improve learning, some tools are embedded with more network learning features, making it easier to connect people, resources, and tools than the others. In general, effective networking tools should be compatible with the features of personalizing, creating, sharing, networking, managing, and mobilizing. One tool may not have all features; however, if one has more than another, you will have a wider range of features to integrate. If necessary, review each chapter for different selection criteria for each linkage design.

To Organize PLE and ONLE

PLE and ONLE are constantly evolving. Effective PLE and ONLE require more than the initial design, development, and creation. The secret to success lies in organizing them regularly based on your changing needs. Remind your students to organize and update their PLE regularly to reflect their personal needs, just as you organize and update your ONLE. This is the best way to maximize learning.

To Share and Collaborate on PLE and ONLE

Effective PLE and ONLE require students and teachers to share their learning network with other learners and teachers and to collaborate with others. This is because PLE and ONLE are "environments"; that is, they are organic and dynamic. You and your students can collaborate with your PLE and ONLE by sharing them with others. Students also learn by constructing their PLE within ONLE. That is the beauty of this system. An ONLE built by you and your students allows all participants to learn and grow and opens the learning to other courses as well. It is not a static course, model, or unit. It is a constantly evolving, organic entity.

To Link Tools to PLE and ONLE

Linking different tools to create your PLE and ONLE is as important as connecting to other people and learning content. It is critical that learners and teachers connect multiple tools within these learning environments, rather than employing them individually as stand-alone learning tools. Effectively linking learning tools applies the open network linkage design model (see Linkage Designs and Learning Activity sections for more details).

COMPREHENSIVE LINKAGE ACTIVITY DESIGNS

To Create PLE and ONLE Activities

Create activities to actively engage learners in PLE and ONLE. These activities could be part of the required instructions, activities, and assignments, or they could be special projects. The activities can be individual and/or collaborative. Some can be integrated into a class or community as collaboration activities. (See the Learning Activity for the suggested highlight activities.)

- Explain to students the value of building PLE and ONLE for your instructions before the class starts. Consider showing them examples of a PLE and an ONLE. If possible, ask any students who have already built their PLEs to share their reflections with others.
- Tell students to create their own PLEs at the beginning of the course. You might also ask them to show and tell how and what they create in their PLEs and in what ways they intend to apply PLEs to support their learning.
- Show and tell of students' PLEs can also be integrated at the mid and the end of the class, since they will be updating and organizing their PLEs throughout the term. This also gives you an opportunity to learn about the students' progress.

COMPREHENSIVE LINKAGE DESIGNS

Besides connecting to tools, people, and resources, the linkage design model can help you design a more effective and comprehensive ONLE. Use each linkage model to design effective activities. It is not necessary to integrate all linkages from the linkage design model, but consider all linkages and explore whether any would be effective in your instructions. Then select the one(s) that are most relevant to your teaching and instructions.

**LEARNING ACTIVITY: COMPREHENSIVE
ONLE LINKAGE DESIGN FOR ONLINE INSTRUCTIONS**

Purpose: This Learning Activity discusses an online course that delivers the entire course instruction on multiple Web 2.0 tools that integrate the concepts of connectivity, PLE, and ONLE. Beyond replacing the LMS, the purpose of integrating PLE and ONLE is to comprehensively integrate design methods and strategies that support effective learning.

Multiple Web 2.0 tools intertwine as ONLE to help you deliver course instruction, as well as to nurture individual learners' PLEs. Each tool is integrated to serve a single or multiple instructional functions (see Table 14.1).

Table 14.1   Integrated Web 2.0 Tools to Support PLE and ONLE (Tu et al., 2012)

Functions	Tools
Management Tools	
Customized personal portal	iGoogle[ab] (or students' choices on PageFlakes; NetVibes)
Learning resources	Google Reader[ab] (or students' choices)
Research/ bibliography	Zotero,[b] Mendeley[b]
Communication Tools	
Announcements	Twitter[ab]
Discussion boards	Wikidiscussion forum,[a] Twitter,[ab] VoiceThread,[a] Diigo,[ab] Nabble, multidimentional discussions[ab] (multiple tools)
E-mail	Gmail[ab]
Web conferencing	Skype,[ab] Elluminate
Mobile learning	Gmail,[ab] Delicious,[ab] Diigo,[ab] Twitter,[ab] Mobl21,[b] Skype,[ab] RSS,[ab] Facebook,[ab] Google Calendar[a]
Course Content/ Instruction Tools	
Course content	Wiki (Wetpaint, Google Sites[ab])
Calendar	Google Calendar[ab]
Schedule	Dipity
Assignment drop box	Google Docs[a]
Blogs	Blogger[ab] (or students' choices) for individual, group, and course blogs.
Production Tools	
Documents	Google Docs[ab]
Presentations	Google Docs' Presentation tool,[ab] Prezi
Mind-mapping	Webspiration, Mindomo, Gliffy, etc. (or students' choices as long as they can be collaborated online)
Collaborative Tools	
Group collaboration	GoogleWave,[ab] Wiki, Google Docs[ab] (or students' choices)

Table 14.1 (Continued)

Distributed Resource Tools	
Bookmarks	Delicious[ab]
Annotations	Diigo[ab]
Multimedia	YouTube[ab]
Bibliographical	Zotero, Mendeley[b]
Social Networking Tools	
Social networking	Facebook,[ab] Twitter[ab]
Information Visualization Tools	
Tag/Word clouds	Wordle
Timeline-based tool	Dipity

[a]Available on iGoogle gadgets
[b]Available on mobile apps

Below are a few PLE and ONLE instructional activities that you can use to enhance network learning experiences.

PLE Setup

Effective PLE requires that students be competent with self-regulation and metacognition skills, so they can create their PLE on iGoogle as their first instructional activity; and manage multiple required and optional course Web 2.0 tools by adding gadgets to their iGoogle page. iGoogle is a customizable personal web portal that can be used to build a PLE. Students may wish to use web portals other than iGoogle, such as RSS readers or Netvibes. Whatever portal they use, PLE setup is critical because in this course they will integrate multiple Web 2.0 tools.

Ask your students to create a new iGoogle tab, named PLE, and to add required course gadgets—such as Twitter, Google Calendar, Google Docs, VoiceThread, Delicious, Google Reader/RSS—to the tabs when you assign them the task of adding optional gadgets. Almost all Web 2.0 tools feature RSS feed capability. With RSS feed subscriptions, students can organize, manage, and monitor their learning content, activities, and resources on Google Reader without visiting actual websites. After the setup, instruct students to visit their iGoogle page regularly to manage their course activities and determine whether any course instructions need attention.

Have students apply mind-mapping tools to create their PLE diagrams, so they can visualize and update/manage their PLEs and share them with the class through tagging them on Delicious. Ask students to review each other's diagrams, make any necessary updates, and reflect on how they might use the PLEs to support their open network learning. At the end of the class, have them discuss their PLE experiences on the value of gadgets and tools applied, describe how they used their PLE, and talk about their overall learning experiences. See different visual examples at http://edtechpost.wikispaces.com/PLE+Diagrams.

Tagging to Build Community

Social tagging architecture can be designed and applied to support students and teachers and help them organize and share their network learning resources (e.g., Delicious and Diigo) to build a network community. Social tagging involves students in fundamental learning skills, analysis, contextualization, and conceptualization. Course social tagging architecture stratifies into two tagging strategies: organization stratum and sharing stratum.

Organization stratum tagging strategies utilize different types of tags that reflect human knowledge and cognition. These include community tags (course number), content tags, instructional activity tags (Assignment1, Module1, etc.), and private tags. Sharing stratum uses collaborative tags to share resources with different components of communities in the network environment, such as community of interest, purpose, passion, and practice.

Have students apply course-tagging schemes to their course assignments, activity resources, and references. Tagging design also allows them to search the learning resources of previous students. The course itself gains context-rich learning resources when students tag to share resources. With effective social tagging architecture, community-community interaction is facilitated seamlessly, enabling community learning in different temporal and spatial locations. This way, upcoming students and instructors can start the class with robust learning resources rather than an empty course shell. In addition, the tagged resources remain available to them after they complete the course. This strategic social tagging architecture authentically achieves the goals of OERs and global digital learning. See the example of social tagging architecture at https://sites.google.com/site/etc655/tagging-architecture.

Collaborative Textbook Creations

In this learning module, student groups, utilizing social-constructive learning, select a lesson topic and collaboratively develop the lesson content to preserve as a course textbook. Chapters are hosted on a wiki for current and future students as required learning content, thus creating a new edition of the course textbook each semester. Based on the principles of OER, these different editions of textbooks can be made available to other global digital citizens as well. This activity engages students in meaningful and authentic learning in UGC and in community-community interaction.

Ask student groups to develop the course textbook chapters based on their readings, the instructor's guidelines, and lesson discussion resources. Encourage them to aggregate and to remix their chapter content from creditable network resources, as well as from the chapter created by previous students, with appropriate and current references. Relevant references and sources can be shared on Delicious with required tag schemes. The course content UGC textbooks residing on the course wiki can be accessed at iTunes U on mobile devices to accommodate mobile learning.

Network Discussions

Remember, ONLE discussions need not be limited to a text-based, threaded discussion format. Creative and effective network discussions can be implemented through single and multiple communication and collaboration technologies to express other ideas and knowledge.

Open Network Discussion Forum

An open network discussion forum is similar to LMS threaded discussion boards; however, open network forums are displayed in a chronological, flat-structured format that contains RSS features. This requires that students master their self-regulation skills and manage flat-structured discussion feeds to their RSS readers, such as Google Reader; or on mobile devices, to monitor discussion activities without visiting actual discussion sites.

Additionally, flat-structured discussions offer tagging features for discussion topics. After replying in a discussion forum, students are required to add new tags/keywords to tag fields based on their new postings, for discussion topics or "Subject" fields of postings. Applying tags to organize network discussions helps support distributed cognition and enhances critical thinking in general (Schellens et. al., 2009).

Multimodality Network Discourses

You need not limit your network discussions to text format. VoiceThread is a multimedia commenting tool that allows students five different ways (texts, audio, video, telephone, and audio files) to post their comments to a discussion topic, whether it be images, documents, or video. Applying a dual-coding learning theory, students are allowed to use their preferred posting method to participate in the network discussions. They can monitor the VoiceThread discussions on their iGoogle page without visiting the actual discussion site.

Ubiquitous Discourse

Twitter is a microblogging tool and is not designed as a forum tool. However, it can be integrated to support network discussion in informal, reflecting, brainstorming, and resource-sharing tasks. To participate in the collaborative Twitter discussion for the course, students should include the course hashtag in their tweets. Because tweets are limited to 140 characters, students must be concise. They can make their postings from mobile devices or any other available tool at any time to enhance context-rich learning. Students can subscribe to RSS feeds on the Twitter discussion hashtag, allowing them to monitor the discussion without visiting Twitter.

Multidimensional Discussions

Thinking is multidimensional and may not always conform to a linear format. Typical online discussion tools focus on one dimension at a time with more formal, threaded postings. Mixed types of postings in single-dimension discussions may result in losing a sense of communication and interaction; and other types of postings may diffuse content. Open network, multidimensional discussion integrates multiple tools to allow students to participate in discussions based on different types of thinking. Multiple network discussion forums, such as Diigo, Delicious, Twitter, wiki, RSS, and iGoogle, empower students and engage them in multiple dimensions of interaction, which mimics their nonlinear, networked thinking. This integration can enhance learning by fostering deeper thinking in cognitive responses.

When students think formally, they can contribute to wiki content or flat-structured discussion board. When they prefer to comment on specific wiki content, they can annotate a specific part of the webpage with Diigo postings, and this can become a new discussion topic. When students wish to engage in more informal reflections or chat, they can tweet their comments with the required hashtag. If they prefer to share learning resources, they can apply the course-required tags to share on Delicious.

Multiple tools could require students to visit multiple web locations to complete network discussions, but with RSS feeds for each discussion tool, they can monitor the discussion as it occurs in multiple dimensions. Network linkage capability permits learners to manage multiple discussion forums from one central location, such as Google Reader or iGoogle, despite the fact that their forum tools are scattered. These postings become students' digital cognition prints (Campbell, 2008b) and digital social identities, and you can even allow them access after the course is completed. Students and instructors can continue participating in discussions via mobile Apps and RSS on mobile devices.

Cloud Collaboration

You can streamline assignment submissions and collaboration for ONLE through cloud computing. In the course, have students complete all assignment submissions via Google Docs. They may submit them by sharing them with instructors, teammates, or classmates as collaborators with editing privilege, or simply as viewers. This approach supports socio-constructive learning theory. As the instructor, you can use Google Docs' commenting feature to provide feedback, comments, and grades. This submission process, utilizing cloud-computing concepts, eliminates downloading and uploading. Both students and instructors can access documents anywhere and anytime without requiring software installation, since they are browser-based tasks. Additionally, students and instructors can publish their documents as webpages to advance distributed learning to another level of OER learning.

Information Visualization (InfoViz)

InfoViz refers to information design that "uses picture, symbols, colors, and words to communicate ideas, illustrate information, or express relationships visually" (Emerson, 2008, p. 4); and it can reduce cognitive load, according to cognitive psychology. Integrate InfoViz to support communication in network discussions and course schedules. Word and tag clouds created on Wordle can be generated every three to four days by student moderators to support network discussions within the InfoViz architecture. This helps you avoid the typical weaknesses of online threaded discussions, that is, less synthesis, losing sight of the discussion topic, and fragmented understanding. InfoViz enhances learning in online discussion, especially with memory and processing capabilities, information search paths, pattern detection, critical information, inferences, and data manipulations (Card et al., 1999). To facilitate course management, a course schedule, generated on Dipity, can be integrated by students through visual and timeline-based tools, rather than adhere to the traditional text-based course schedule.

LAST WORDS

Social tagging resources can be seen on Delicious in chapter 1, Table 1.1.

PLE empowers learners to make their learning more personal, connected, social, networked, and open. Students usually appreciate that ONLE allows them make their PLEs more personal by permitting them to develop more and better personal and team-centered content and to select their preferred tools from wide range of tools. Connective design and linking multiple tools allow students to share and connect to information more socially, effectively, and efficiently, and to more easily manage their PLEs. These tools are personally selected by the students and need not be limited to those recommended by the instructor.

Open network design enables students to build an authentic, network learning community through context-rich social interaction rather than focusing on content only. Students should be able to project more positive social digital identities and become proficient network community learners. With network design, cloud computing distributes learning ubiquitously, supporting learning anywhere and anytime. Students who use smartphones or mobile devices understand that they can actively engage in learning whenever and wherever they prefer. With personalized seamless authentication, iGoogle resolves multiple tools and account signing-in issues, even when not using their own device. With OER design, students have the ability to access learning course materials after finishing the course. They can continue learning from the course's open resources, and their digital content creations and contributions become their digital cognition print.

As instructor, you will undoubtedly value the design of networked collaborative learning community. ONLE facilitates community learning that supports community-community interaction and allows the community/ course to continue learning, term after term. Students take on more responsibility for their learning and practice decision making individually and collectively, as well as becoming engaged in content creation and contribution for other students. ONLE experiences align better with effective community and collaborations instructional designs. With ONLE and PLE design, you should notice that students become true global digital citizens by creating, sharing, and collaborating on learning content and resources ranging from individual and course levels to a global community. Students develop the understanding that they are fundamental to making a global digital community a better environment for all learners.

CHAPTER 15

Finis

ADVANCE ONLINE LEARNERS TO NETWORK LEARNERS

Technology disrupts learning, and today, Web 2.0 learning environments are disrupting LMSs. Online learning proponents should reflect on the past and look to the future to establish effective online learning for the future. PLEs and ONLEs offer online learners the opportunity to learn by acting within a system they have helped create, using interaction with other students to accomplish their learning goals. Open network linkage design model skills are critical to establishing PLEs and ONLEs. Simply giving multiple Web 2.0 tools to learners and instructors does not result in effective PLE and ONLE. It is your responsibility as an educator to prepare and assist network learners in building social network linkage skills, so they are able to successfully achieve network learning.

As an educator, you have the opportunity to prepare and advance online learners to become network learners. The two are different. Network learners in ONLE do not just consume learning content; they create and edit learning content collaboratively with other network learners. Additionally, while creating and editing content collaboratively, network learners "aggregate," "mash up," and "remix" identified network learning content to generate a new set of content with their creative ideas to personalize their learning.

Higher education is currently transitioning from online learning to an ONLE. Online learners use their mental, distributed learning model to make sense of their "network" learning mental model. As a consequence, these learners do not comprehend the value that social network interaction with

ONLE offers; rather, they see ONLE as just another online learning environment. These learners may not be able to comprehend how "online" interaction is related to ONLE's network interaction. If online learners cannot comprehend the values of ONLE's social interaction, it is challenging for them to learn how to be "network" learners, which requires more specific social interaction in cognitive interaction (creating, editing, remixing, and sharing social content) and social interaction (build and maintain digital and social identities).

In a constructivist and connectivist learning context, both teachers and students are learners. By integrating the open network linkage design model, and creating and cocreating ONLE with network learners to assist all network learners to build their PLEs, online instructors have an opportunity to advance themselves to network instructors.

FACING THE CHALLENGES

Integrating PLE and ONLE is not without challenges. The PLE and ONLE are not panaceas for education. To integrate them effectively, you must first have a good understanding of the challenges as well as the benefits. Below are a few challenges that you should prepare yourself to face and to resolve.

Mental Model Shifting

Many students and teachers are accustomed to broadcast or hierarchical learning (or mental models), rather than network linkage. Both students and teachers could fail because they fear managing open network linkages. In fact, it is fairly common for some to apply traditional teaching and learning methods and access each tool individually in the complicated PLE and ONLE. The key to mental model shifting is managing the multitools learning environment.

Changes in Procedures and Processes

Additionally, both students and teachers must prepare for problem solving, because Web 2.0 tools are evolving constantly. Their features may come and go, or be updated. Procedures and processes required to perform certain functions may be different at the time you are integrating than when the course started. The key is to understand overall design concepts, constructs, and frameworks: connectivism (Siemens, 2005), constructs for Web 2.0 learning environments (Tu, Blocher, and Roberts, 2008), PLE (van Harmelen, 2006a and 2006b), and ONLE (Tu et al., 2012). Network technologies may be evolving, but if you have a general understanding of these, you will be able to apply your knowledge to evaluate any emerging tools and technologies and to integrate them effectively.

Missing Self-Regulatory Skills

Students and teachers are accustomed to being told what to do and what to learn, rather than being allowed to determine their learning goals and manage how they learn. In traditional classrooms, students are not given opportunities to organize their own learning; therefore, they are not accustomed to organizing and managing their PLE. In other words, their self-regulatory skills are missing. Educators should prepare network learners to obtain self-regulatory learning skills, strategy, and knowledge before any content learning can occur. Educators should constantly remind network learners to improve their self-regulatory skills throughout the network learning process.

Frustrations

With learners accustomed to using a single learning tool or technology, it is common that they become frustrated when asked to use multiple tools. The new social media tools require an increased ability to cope with a range of different tools. The educator should coach and model the integration of the multitools learning environment.

Support

Often, integrating multiple tools into a course results in noncentralized technical support for students and teachers. Generally, educational institutions do not support Web 2.0 tools, since they do not host and own the tools and operations. In fact, frequently, they are banned at primary and secondary education institutions because of safety and security concerns. Educators should consult with the institution technology support group and demonstrate leadership in emerging technology integration to the institution.

Distracting

Many educators worry that integrating multiple tools will distract students from learning. Educators are still debating whether utilizing multiple tools and multitasking will have negative effects. However, integrating multiple tools simultaneously has been proven to be the best strategy for learning (Dede, 2008). So the network learner should be instructed to learn this strategy.

Adapting

It is unfair to expect that all students and teachers will be able to adapt to multiple Web 2.0 tools immediately. Educators often wrongly assume that digital native generations will have no trouble with adopting and adapting to emerging technologies. In fact, even if they are familiar with these network technologies, not all students are able to use them as new learning tools. Keep in mind that all students and teachers need time to adapt to this new approach to learning. If the learner has difficulty in adapting to a multi-tools learning environment, she should begin with one or two tools and add others as she become comfortable, rather than using a full span of tools in the beginning.

Attitude

When learning new skills and knowledge, it is critical that learners have a positive attitude toward emerging learning paradigms and are willing to try new tools and experience trial and error. Be sure the learner has a good understanding of the new paradigm.

Safety and Security Concerns

Safety and security concerns are major issues to educators. Because of the shift of control from educators and educational institutions to learners, educators, parents, and other relevant stakeholders often express these concerns about open, social, and network learning environments. Not all students have a firm understanding of network learning environments. Incidents such as inappropriate digital access, cyberbullying, improper digital etiquette, unhealthy digital wellness, and digital security breaching may occur frequently. Before implementing PLE and ONLE, discuss safety and security concerns of network learning with the students. Dabbs (2012) suggests five building blocks to ensure educators have appropriate network learning integration for teaching, learning, and connecting with students and parents: notify parents, develop a responsible use policy, establish classroom management procedures, plan activities with students, and teach safety and etiquette.

Accessibility Issues

Accessibility is another issue to be examined while selecting any emerging technologies. Not all emerging tools comply with Section 508 Amendment to the Rehabilitation of Act of 1973 that was enacted to eliminate barriers in information technology, to make available new opportunities for people with disabilities, and to encourage development of technologies, such as universal design (UD) and assistive technology. Accessibility for each Web 2.0 tool must be confirmed before using them. If the Web 2.0 website did not disclaim accessibility, be sure to contact the company that has provided the tool.

FROM NETWORK LEARNERS TO GLOBAL DIGITAL CITIZENS

Network learning focuses on content creation, sharing, managing, and collaboration; however, to resolve the challenging issues discussed above, network learners should advance themselves as competent global digital citizens. Tu and McIsaac (in press) suggest a model to prepare global digital citizens by implementing five dimensions of identity grounded in a sociocultural constructivist pedagogy, six enabling processes, and three catalytic forces in the process of fully becoming a global digital citizen. To implement the five dimensions, educators should prepare a digital learner to become a social collaborator, cultural constructivist, community collaborator, and finally global digital citizen. The learner progresses from being a digital learner through social, cultural, and environmental levels, developing the skills required to move through each level of the five dimensions, finally arriving at the level of global digital citizen.

During this progression, educators can increase the momentum and enable the individual's progress through the five dimensions toward the goal of global digital citizen with six enablers. These six enabling processes are networking, mobilizing, sharing, creating, personalizing, and managing.

Finally, three catalysts, which can be visualized as spiraling forces, can be activated to increase the momentum of the individual's progress. These digital agents are based on the sociocultural concepts in linguistics and semiotics of instrumental tools, semiotic tools, and premediated tools. The catalysts are digital devices, digital communication applications, and digital management environments.

Promoting an open network learning environment does not exclude learning in the physical world. In fact, the digital learning world extends real-world learning environments. While we support and advocate globalization in the real world, shouldn't our digital PLE and ONLE be at the digital global level? Learning may be personal, but true learning is global. Master Cheng-Yen teaches: A true self is selfless.

GLOSSARY

Augmented reality (AR): is a live, direct or indirect, view of a physical, real-world environment whose elements are augmented by computer-generated sensory input such as sound, video, graphics, or Global Positioning System data.

Connectivism: Connective learning is the process of establishing connections that enable learners to acquire knowledge and learn more. This focus recognizes the fact that learning is based on the idea that "rapidly altering foundations ... currency (accurate, up-to-date knowledge) is the intent of all connectivist learning activities" (Siemens, 2005).

Digital identity: Digital identities are created voluntarily and involuntarily, since many actions and activities are recorded in digital forms and can be retrieved online without one actually being created.

Digital social identity: Digital social identities include the shared social content and social communications occurring on social network sites that are recorded and become the digital social footprint. Generally, this type of communication is called "feeds" and is more like a person's face value.

Feed (web): A web feed (or news feed) is a data format used for providing learners with regularly updated content. Content distributors syndicate a web feed, thus allowing learners to subscribe to it.

Flat-structured discussion board: applies a simple interface; all postings are displayed in a single level, rather than in a threaded or nested reply structure.

Hashtag: refers to a word or phrase prefixed with the symbol "#" (i.e., hashtag). A hashtag has the function of creating groupings on Twitter. This enables tweets to be categorized based on a particular topic.

Information visualization (InfoViz): or InfoGraphic refers to information design that "uses picture, symbols, colors, and words to communicate ideas, illustrate information, or express relationships visually" (Emerson, 2008, p. 4).

iOS (internetwork Operation System): is Apple's mobile operation system. It is developed for Apple's mobile devices, such as iPhone, iPad, and iPod Touch.

Learning management system (LMS): is a software application for the administration, documentation, tracking, reporting, and delivery of education courses, content, instructions, or training programs, such as Blackboard Learning or Moodle.

Mobile application (mobile app): is a software application designed to run on smartphones, tablet computers, and other mobile devices.

Mobile linkage: refers to using mobile apps to link to Web 2.0 tools on mobile devices. Mobile linkage involves more than using an Internet browser to access online information. Specifically, by employing mobile apps, mobile linkage focuses on controlling social context awareness, managing location-based communication, personalized multilayered interactivity, and optimized digital and social identities.

Open educational resources (OER): are openly licensed learning and teaching instructions, content, and resources for universal access.

Open network learning environment (ONLE): is a digital environment that empowers learners to participate in creative endeavors, conduct social networking, organize and reorganize social contents, and manage social acts by connecting people, resources, and tools by integrating Web 2.0 tools to design environments that are totally transparent, or open to public view. This same architecture can be used to design the degree of transparency users feel is necessary to the situation.

Open network linkage design model: refers to a "linkage architecture" that "links and connects" multiple network resources, network learners, and Web 2.0 tools in ONLE to allow learners, instructors, and other ONLE stakeholders to construct and share their PLEs within a human network.

Personal learning environment (PLE): is a new technology that enables individuals to personalize the environment in which they learn by connecting and managing learning networks. By appropriating a range of tools, and by connecting people, resources, and tools, they are able to meet their learning interests and needs.

Personal portal linkage: is a customized portal technology that links multiple Web 2.0 tools in one location and allows learners and instructors to manage their learning content, information, and communications.

RSS (RDF site summary, rich site summary, or really simple syndication): is simple XML syntax for portraying recent additions of content to a website. It allows online learners to independently subscribe to their choice of content and sources across the web, thus reducing the need for users to visit many individual websites.

RSS linkage: refers to the application of an RSS feed from one tool to others so learners can monitor or track a single place to get updates through live feeds.

Social network linkage: refers to learners connecting to online social networks, by becoming friends or fans of others, or following others via Web 2.0 tools to build social relationships and to get updated on friends' learning resources and so forth. By becoming members of social networks, users are granted privileges to view more of their friends' resources and their social networks.

Social network sites (SNS): connect people and support different communities of practice. The openness and malleability of use of these tools empowers users to express themselves to others, and to take part in shared activities, in a variety of contexts.

Social tagging linkage: refers to social tags that link relevant content, networked friends/fans, and community. Many tools have social tagging features, such as Delicious, Flickr, Diigo, blog postings, and wiki discussion postings.

Third-party linkage: refers to the application of third-party tools (such as Google Sync, Google Cloud Connect for Microsoft Office, Twitterfeed, TwitterDeck, Permalink, Google +, Patchlife, and Posterous) to link multiple Web 2.0 tools, so content or resources can be streamed from one tool to other tools. Generally, a third-party linkage tool works behind the scenes, so it is not apparent to users.

User-generated content (UGC): describes any form of web content—such as video, blog, discussion form posts, digital images, audio files, and other forms of media—that was created by learners of an online system or service and is publically available to others learners.

Widget linkage: refers to a stand-alone that can be embedded into another tool by learners or instructors on a webpage where they have rights of authorship (e.g., a webpage, blog, or profile on a social media site).

ACRONYMS

Apps	application
AR	augmented reality
CMC	computer-mediated communication
CMS	course management system
FTF	face to face
GPS	Global Position System
IFTTT	If This Then That
InfoGraph	information graphic
InfoViz	information vitalization
LMS	learning management system
ML	mobile learning
MMR	multimodality representation
OER	open educational resource
ONLE	open network learning environment
OS	operation system
PDF	portable document format
PLE	personal learning environment
RSS	RDF site summary, rich site summary, or really simple syndication
SNL	social network linkage
SNS	social network site

UD	universal Design
UGC	user-generated content
URL	uniform resource locator
XML	extensible markup language

REFERENCES

Alexander, B. (2006). Web 2.0: A new wave of innovation for teaching and learning? *EDUCAUSE Review*, *41*(2), 32–44.

Augmented reality. (n.d.). In *Wikipedia*. Retrieved from http://en.wikipedia.org/wiki/Augmented_reality

Barnard-Brak, L., Lan, W. Y., & Paton, V. O. (2010). Profiles in self-regulated learning in the online learning environment. *The International Review of Research in Open and Distance Learning*, *11*(1). Retrieved from http://www.irrodl.org/index.php/irrodl/article/view/769/1480

Barron, B. (2006). Interest and self-sustained learning as catalysts of development: A learning ecologies perspective. *Human Development*, *49*, 193–224.

Blazer, C. (2012). *Social networking in schools: Benefits and risks; Review of the research; policy considerations; and current practices. Information Capsule* (No. 1109). Miami-Dade: Miami-Dade County Public Schools.

Bonk, C., & Dennen, V. (2007). Frameworks for design and instruction. In M. G. Moore (Ed.), *Handbook of distance education* (2nd ed., pp. 233–246). Mahwah, NJ: Lawrence Erlbaum Associates.

Boyd, D. M., & Ellison, N. B. (2007). Social network sites: Definition, history, and scholarship. *Journal of Computer-Mediated Communication*, *13*(1), article 11.

Braun, S., & Schmidt, A. (2000). Socially-aware informal learning support: Potentials and challenges of the social dimension. *Proceedings of the European Conference on Technology-Enhanced Learning (EC-TEL 06)*. Heraklion, October 2006. Retrieved from http://publications.professional-learning.eu/Schmidt_Braun_LOKMOL06_final.pdf

Brown, J. S. (1999). Learning, working, and playing in the digital age. *Presented at the American Association for Higher Education Conference on Higher Education*. Washington, DC. Retrieved from http//www.ntlf.com/html/sf/jsbrown.pdf

Bush, M., & Mott, J. (2009). The transformation of learning with technology learner-centricity, content and tool malleability, and network effects. *Educational Technology, 49*(2), 3–20.

Campbell, G. (2008a, March 1). Web 2.0 in education. Retrieved March 1, 2009, from http://blip.tv/file/1447489

Campbell, G. (2008b, November 9). Cognition prints. *Gardner Wires.* Blog. Retrieved from http://www.gardnercampbell.net/blog1/?p=635

Card, S. K., Mackinlay, J. D., & Shneiderman, B. (1999). *Readings in information visualization: Using vision to think.* San Francisco: Morgan Kaufmann.

Carotenuto, L., Etienne, W., Fontaine, M., Friedman, J., Muller, M., Newberg, H., Simpson, M., et al. (1999). CommunitySpace: Toward flexible support for voluntary knowledge communities. *Paper presented at Changing Places workshop.* London, UK. Retrieved from http://domino.watson.ibm.com/cambridge/research.nsf/0/0e8c8166a02d5338852568f800634af1/$FILE/communityspace.PDF

Charlton, T., Devlin, M., & Drummond, S. (2009). Using Facebook to improve communication in undergraduate software development teams. *Computer Science Education, 19*(4), 273–292.

Cheong, C. M., & Cheung, W. S. (2008). Online discussion and critical thinking skills: A case study in a Singapore secondary school. *Australasian Journal of Educational Technology, 24*(5), 556–573.

Chi, E. H. (2002). *A framework for visualizing information.* New York: Springer.

Clarke, D. J., & Jennings, C. (2009). Experiential learning: Bringing knowledge to life. Retrieved from http://toolwire.com/files/ExperientialLearning.pdf

Coiro, J., Knobel, M., Lankshear, C., & Leu, D. (2008). Central issues in new literacies and new literacies research. In J. Coiro, M. Knobel, C. Lankshear, & D. Leu (Eds.), *Central issues in new literacies and new literacies research.* New York: Lawrence Erlbaum Associates.

Conole, G. (2008). New schemas for mapping pedagogies and technologies. *Ariadne,* (56). Retrieved from http://www.ariadne.ac.uk/issue56/conole/

Conole, G., & Culver, J. (2010). The design of Cloudworks: Applying social networking practice to foster the exchange of learning and teaching ideas and designs. *Computers & Education, 54*(3), 679–692.

Cornelius, S., & Marston, P. (2009). Toward an understanding of the virtual context in mobile learning. *Research in Learning Technology, 17*(3), 161–172.

Dabbs, L. (2012, October 25). Mobile learning support for new teachers. *Teaching with Soul.* Blog. Retrieved November 15, 2012, from http://www.teachingwithsoul.com/2012/mobile-learning-support-for-new-teachers

De Leng, B. A., Dolmans, D. H. J. M., Jobsis, R., Muijtjens, A. M. M., and van der Vleuten, C. P. M. (2009). Exploration of an e-learning model to foster critical thinking on basic science concepts during work placements. *Computers & Education, 53*(1), 1–13.

Dede, C. (2008). Theoretical perspectives influencing the use of information technology in teaching and learning. In J. Voogt & G. Knezek (Eds.), *International handbook of information technology in primary and secondary education.* New York: Springer.

Educause. (2008). 2008 Horizon Report. Retrieved September 22, 2008, from http://connect.educause.edu/Library/ELI/2008HorizonReport/45926?time=1224635003

Ellison, N. B., Steinfield, C., & Lampe, C. (2007). The benefits of Facebook "friends": Social capital and college students' use of online social network sites. *Journal of Computer-Mediated Communication*, 12(4).

Emerson, J. (2008). Visualization information for advocacy: An introduction to information design. Retrieved March 1, 2010, from http://backspace.com/infodesign.pdf

Faculty Focus. (2009). *Twitter in higher education: Usage habits and trends of today's college faculty*. Madison, MI. Retrieved from http://www.facultyfocus.com/free-report/twitter-in-higher-education-usage-habits-and-trends-of-todays-college-faculty/

Feinberg, J. (2013). *Wordle*. Retrieved from http://www.wordle.net/

Feldstein, M. (2005, March 30). Threaded discussion interfaces: A research challenge. *e_literate*. Retrieved from http://mfeldstein.com/threaded_discussion_interfaces_a_research_challenge/

Ganiz, F. (2009). *"Social learning" buzz masks deeper dimensions: Mitigating the confusion surrounding "Social Learning."* General Partner, Gilfus Education Group. Retrieved from http://www.gilfuseducationgroup.com/social-learning-buzz-masks-deeper-dimensions

Garrison, D. R., Anderson, T., & Archer, W. (2001). Critical thinking and computer conferencing: A model and tool to access cognitive presence. *American Journal of Distance Education*, 15, 7–23.

Godwin-Jones, R. (2006). Tag clouds in the blogosphere: Electronic literacy and social networking. *Language Learning & Technology*, 10(2), 8–15.

Greenhow, C., Robelia, B., & Hughes, J. E. (2009). Learning, teaching, and scholarship in a digital age: Web 2.0 and classroom research: What path should we take now? *Educational Researcher*, 38, 246–259.

Hall, M. (2009). Towards a fusion of formal and informal learning environments: The Impact of the read/write web. *Electronic Journal of e-Learning*, 7(1), 29–40.

Herrington, J., Reeves, T., & Oliver, R. (2005). Online learning as information delivery: Digital myopia. *Journal of Interactive Learning Research*, 16(4), 353–367.

Hillman, D. C. A., Willis, D. J., & Gunawardena, C. N. (1994). Learner-interface interaction in distance education: An extension of contemporary models and strategies for practitioners. *American Journal of Distance Education*, 8(2), 30–42.

Jones, A., & Issroff, K. (2007). Motivation and mobile devices: Exploring the role appropriation and coping strategies. *Research in Learning Technology*, 15(3), 247–258.

Jones, N., Blackey, H., Fitzgibbon, K., & Chew, E. (2010). Get out of MySpace! *Computers & Education*, 54(3), 776–782.

Kekwaletswe, R. M. (2007). Social presence awareness for knowledge transformation in a mobile learning environment. *International Journal of Education and Development Using Information and Communication Technology*, 3(4), 102–109.

Keller, T., Gerjets, P., Scheiter, K., & Garsoffky, B. (2005). Information visualizations for knowledge acquisition. *Computers in Human Behavior, 22*, 43–65.

Komando, K. (2012, January 5). Four digital resolutions for 2012. *USA Today.* Retrieved from http://usatoday30.usatoday.com/tech/columnist/kimkomando/story/2012-01-06/2012-tech-resolutions/52391568/1

Koole, M., McQuilkin, J. L., & Ally, M. (2010). Mobile learning in distance education: Utility or futility? *Journal of Distance Education, 24*(2), 59–82.

Kukulska-Hulme, A., & Traxler, J. (2007). Learning design with mobile and wireless technologies. In H. Beetham & R. Sharpe (Eds.), *Rethinking pedagogy for a digital age: Designing and delivering e-learning* (pp. 180–192). London, UK. Retrieved from http://oro.open.ac.uk/9541/

Lee, J. J., & Hammer, J. (2011). Gamification in education: What, how, why bother? *Academic Exchange Quarterly, 15*(2). Retrieved from http://www.gamifyingeducation.org/files/Lee-Hammer-AEQ-2011.pdf

Lee, M. J. W., Miller, C., & Newnham, L. (2008). RSS and content syndication in higher education: Subscribing to a new model of teaching and learning. *Educational Media International, 45*(4), 311–322.

Lohmann, S., Ziegler, J., & Tetzlaff, L. (2009). Comparison of tag Cloud layouts: Task-related performance and visual exploration.*INTERACT 2009, Part I, LNCS 5726* (pp. 392–404).

Martin, J. (2004). Self-regulated learning, social cognitive theory, and agency. *Educational Psychologist, 39*(3), 135–145.

Morrison, J. (2008). Tagging and searching: Search retrieval effectiveness of folksonomies on the World Wide Web. *Information Processing & Management, 44*(4), 1562–1579.

Mott, J., & Wiley, D. (2009). Open for learning: The CMS and the open learning network. *Technology & Social Media, 15*(2). Retrieved from http://ineducation.ca/article/open-learning-cms-and-open-learning-network

Perkins, D. N. (1993). Person-plus: A distributed view of thinking and learning. *Distributed cognitions: Psychological and educational considerations* (pp. 88–110). Cambridge, UK: Cambridge University Press.

Powell, S. (2006, June 14). Personal learning environments experts meeting. *Thoughts mostly about learning.* Blog. Retrieved from http://www.stephenp.net/2006/06/14/personal-learning-environments-experts-meeting/

Rau, P.-L. P., Gao, Q., & Wu, L.-M. (2008). Using mobile communication technology in high school education: Motivation, pressure, and learning performance. *Computers and Education, 50*(1), 1–22.

Richardson, J. C., & Ice, P. (2010). Investigating students' level of critical thinking across instructional strategies in online discussions. *Internet and Higher Education, 13*(1–2), 52–59.

Schellens, T., Van Keer, H., De Wever, B., & Valcke, M. (2009). Tagging thinking types in asynchronous discussion groups: Effects on critical thinking. *Interactive Learning Environments, 17*(1), 77–94.

Schrock, K. (2012). Bloomin' Apps. Retrieved July 1, 2012, from http://www.schrockguide.net/bloomin-apps.html

Sclater, N. (2008). Web 2.0, personal learning environments, and the future of learning management systems. *ECAR, 2008*(13). Retrieved from http://www.educause.edu/ECAR/Web20PersonalLearningEnvironme/163047

Selwyn, N. (2009). Faceworking: Exploring students' education-related use of Facebook. *Learning, Media and Technology, 34*(2), 157–174.

Sharples, M. (2002). Disruptive devices: Mobile technology for conversational learning. *International Journal of Continuing Engineering Education and Lifelong Learning, 12*(5/6), 505–520.

Siemens, G. (2005). Connectivism: A learning theory for the digital age. *International Journal of Instructional Technology & Distance Learning, 2* (1). Retrieved from http://www.itdl.org/Journal/Jan_05/article01.htm

Siemens, G. (2007). PLEs—I acronym, therefore I exist. *elearnspace.* Retrieved July 9, 2009, from http://www.elearnspace.org/blog/2007/04/15/ples-i-acronym -therefore-i-exist/

Siemens, G., & Cormier, D. (2009, July 8). Social media: Trends and implications for learning. Retrieved July 8, 2009, from http://aace.org/GlobalU/seminars/socialmedia/

Siemens, G., & Matheos, K. (2010). Systemic changes in higher education. *Technology & Social Media, 16*(1). Retrieved from http://ineducation.ca/article/systemic-changes-higher-education

Slagter van Tyron, P. J., & Bishop, M. J. (2009). Theoretical foundations for enhancing social connectedness in online learning environments. *Distance Education, 3*(3), 291–315.

Spencer, R. (2007). *Information visualization: Design for interaction* (2nd ed.). Upper Saddle River, NJ: Prentice Hall.

Stern, S. (2007). Producing sites, exploring identities: Youth online authorship. In D. Buckingham (Ed.). *The John D. and Catherine T. MacArthur Foundation Series on Digital Media and Learning: Youth, identity and digital media* (pp. 95–118). Cambridge, MA: MIT Press. Retrieved from http://www.mitpressjournals.org/toc/dmal/-/6?cookieSet=1

Suess, J., & Morooney, K. (2009). Identity management and trust services: Foundations for cloud computing. *EDUCAUSE Review, 44*(5), 24–26, 28, 32, 34, 38, 40, 42.

Tu, C. H., & Blocher, M. (2010). Web 2.0 learning environments in distance learning. In R. Papa (Ed.), *Technology leadership for school improvement.* Thousand Oaks, CA: Sage Publications.

Tu, C.-H., Blocher, J. M., & Gallagher, L. (2010). Asynchronous network discussions as organizational scaffold learning: Threaded vs. flat-structured discussion boards. *Journal of Educational Technology Development and Exchange, 3*(1), 43–56.

Tu, C.-H., Blocher, M., & Roberts, G. (2008). Constructs for Web 2.0 learning environments: A theatrical metaphor. *Educational Media International, 45*(3), 253–268.

Tu, C.-H. & McIsaac, M., (in press). Faculty support for meeting cultural challenges in online learning. In I. June & C. N. Gunawardena (Eds.), *Culture and online learning.*

Tu, C.-H., Sujo-Montes, L., Yen, C.-J., & Chan, J.-Y. (2012). The integration of personal learning environments & open network learning environments. *TechTrends, 56*(3), 13–19.

Tufte, E. (1997). *Visual explanations: Images and quantities, evidence and narrative.* Cheshire, CT: Graphics Press.

van Harmelen, M. (2006a). Personal learning environments (pp. 815–816). *Presented at the Proceedings of the Sixth International Conference on Advanced Learning Technologies (ICALT'06)*, Kerkrade, The Netherlands: IEEE Computer Society. Retrieved from http://octette.cs.man.ac.uk/jitt/index.php/ Personal_Learning_Environments

van Harmelen, M. (2006b). Personal learning environments. *Personal learning environments*. Retrieved March 1, 2009, from http://octette.cs.man.ac.uk/~mark/ docs/MvH_PLEs_ICALT.pdf

Vonderwell, S., Liang, X., & Alderman, K. (2007). Asynchronous discussions and assessment in online learning. *Journal of Research on Technology in Education*, 39(3), 309–328.

Ware, C. (2004). *Information visualization: Perception of design* (2nd ed.). San Francisco: Morgan Kaufmann.

Weller, M. (2007a, June 12). The Ed Techie: My personal work/leisure/learning environment. *The Ed Techie*. Retrieved from http://nogoodreason.typepad.co.uk/ no_good_reason/2007/12/my-personal-wor.html

Weller, M. (2007b, August 11). The Ed Techie: The VLE/LMS is dead. *The Ed Techie*. Retrieved from http://nogoodreason.typepad.co.uk/no_good_reason/ 2007/11/the-vlelms-is-d.html

Weller, M. (2010). The centralisation dilemma in educational IT. *Journal of Virtual & Personal Learning Environments*, 1(1), 1–9.

Wesch, M. (2009, January 7). From knowledgable to knowledge-able: Learning in new media environments. Academic Commons. Retrieved from http://www .academiccommons.org/commons/essay/knowledgable-knowledge-able

Wetzker, R., Zimmermann, C. C., & Bauckhage, C. (2008). Analyzing social bookmarking systems: A del.icio.us cookbook. In *Proceedings of the ECAI 2008 Mining Social Data Workshop* (pp. 26–30).

Whiteman, J. A. M. (2002). Interpersonal communication in computer mediated learning.

Wu, W. G., & Li, J. (2007). RSS made easy: A basic guide for librarians. *Medical Reference Services Quarterly*, 26(1), 37–50.

Zhao, C., & Kuh, G. D. (2004). Added value: Learning communities and student engagement. *Research in Higher Education*, 45, 115–138.

Zimmerman, B. J. (1998). Academic studying and the development of personal skill: A self-regulatory perspective. *Educational Psychologist*, 33, 73–86.

INDEX

About the Author

CHIH-HSIUNG TU, PhD, is a professor at Northern Arizona University, Flagstaff, and an educational and instructional technology consultant with experience in distance education, open network learning, technology training in teacher education, online learning community, learning organization, and global digital learning. His research interests are distance education, sociocognitive learning, sociocultural learning, online learning community, learning organization, social media, personal learning environments, and network learning environments. He has published more than 75 articles, book chapters, edited a book, authored two books, received multiple honors as keynote speaker, worked in professional development, done professional conference presentations, and more. He has served as an executive board member for ICEM (International Council for Educational Media), SICET (Society for International Chinese in Educational Technology), and International Division at AECT (Association for Educational Communication and Technology). Dr. Tu has global experience with international scholars from Turkey, Portugal, Singapore, Taiwan, Hong Kong, China, Chile, Japan, Niger and Cyprus.